Active Assemblies

Through the year

Ian Addis

LONGMAN

Acknowledgements

We are grateful to the following for permission to reproduce photographs.

John Arnison page 149; Circa Photo Library page 37; Hulton Getty page 24; Tom Miles Photographic page 63; Christine Osborne page 89; © John Walmsley pages 78, 131, 179; © Janine Wiedel Photolibrary page 5.

Cover photograph: © Bubbles/Jennie Woodcock.

Thanks are extended to the lengthy list of individuals and institutions who gave so generously of their time and resources. Without their help *Active Assemblies Through the Year* may never have seen the light of day, and certainly not in its final user-friendly form.

Chris Richards and Frances Le Pla (Northamptonshire Inspection and Advisory Service), Northamptonshire Multicultural Service, Dave Blake, Jane Rose and Sue Perry, Peter Morrell, Andrew Phillips, Robert Mercer, Gus Horsepool (The Mobile Education Project, Leicester), Cynthia Duckworth, David Heggie and John Kemp (Barton Seagrave Primary School), Highfields Primary, Kettering, Cottingham CE Primary, Thorplands Lower, Cedar Road Infant, Arbours Lower, Abingdon Vale Lower, Parklands Middle, Northampton, Raunds Windmill Primary, Oakway Infant, St Barnabas CE Infant, Croyland Road Infant, Our Lady's RC Junior, Victoria Junior, Wellingborough, Finedon Mulso Junior, Meadowside Junior, Burton Latimer, Farthinghoe Primary, The Grange Junior, Daventry, Dave Rzeznik and Mina Parma (Spinney Hill Junior, Leicester), Marilyn Barnes (Nicholas Hawksmoor Primary, Towcester), Exeter Junior, Danesholme Infant, Studfall Junior, Woodnewton Way Junior, Corby, Loatlands Primary, Desborough, Loddington CE Primary, and especially Sue Spooner (Geddington CE Primary), whose advice, encouragement and professional overview proved invaluable throughout the compilation of material.

We are grateful to the following for permission to reproduce copyright material:

the editor, Elaine Abrahams for *TOPIWALO THE HATMAKER*, edited by Elaine Abrahams, published by Harmony Publishing Ltd with text in English with Gujerati, Urdu, Punjabi and Bengali and accompanied by a dual-language cassette; the author, Moira Andrew for her poem 'Museum Piece' © Moira Andrew, first published in *ASSEMBLIES* Scholastic 1994. compiled by Ian Addis and Susan Spooner; Anglia Young Books, Saffron Walden, Essex for stories 'Stone Moses' by Ian Addis from *RICH PICKINGS BOOK ONE: Assembly Stories For Use in the Autumn Term* by Ian Addis, 'Operation Springclean' by Ian Addis from *RICH PICKINGS BOOK TWO: Assembly Stories For Use in the Autumn Term* by Ian Addis; authors' agents for an extract from *CARRIE'S WAR* by Nina Bawden, published Victor Gollancz; A & C Black for stories 'The Chipko Movement' by Jill Brand , 'Yhi, the Mother of the Earth' (adapted) from *THE GREEN UMBRELLA*, 1991; the author, Gina Douthwaite for her poem 'Birth': BBC Enterprises/EMI Music Publishing Ltd, London WC2H OEA for song and score 'One Day' by Susan Stevens © 1980; Durham Music Ltd for song and score to 'Leave Them a Flower' by Wally Whyton. © 1969 by Wally Whyton; Faber & Faber Ltd. for the story 'Melanie Brown and the New Class' by Pamela Oldfield in *MELANIE BROWN AND THE BAG OF SWEETS*, 1974. author's agent for poem 'There isn't Time' by Eleanor Farjeon from *SILVER, SAND & SNOW*, published by David Fulton Publishers Ltd for the stories 'Tinned Pineapple' & 'Carla's Gift' by Ian Addis from *WHAT CAN THE MATTER BE?* 1992. HarperCollins Ltd for poem 'Arthur the Fat Boy' by Gareth Owen from *SONG OF THE CITY*, Fontana Young Lions Originals, 1985; the author, Mike Hoy for his poem 'Books'. © 1994 Mike Hoy; the authors, Sandra Palmer & Elizabeth Breuilly for adapted versions of the stories 'Guru Nanak' & 'Prince Siddhartha' from *A TAPESTRY OF TALES* (Collins Educational); Random House UK Ltd for story 'How Anansi got his Stories' by Floella Benjamin from *WHY THE AGOUTI HAS NO TAIL AND OTHER STORIES*, 1984; authors' agents on behalf of the James Reeves Estate for poem 'Fireworks' by James Reeves from *COMPLETE POEMS FOR CHILDREN* (Heinemann). © James Reeves; Scholastic Educational Ltd for the stories 'Ben's Flowers' by Ian Addis, 'A Special Friend' & 'The Tooth' by Ian Addis (as Charles Marlow) all in *ASSEMBLIES* - Scholastic Collections (1994) compiled by Ian Addis and Sue Spooner; the author, Arthur Scholey for an adaptation into play script of his story 'Elleni and the Sharing Bread' first published in *THE JOHNNY MORRIS STORY BOOK* (BBC Publications); Stainer & Bell Ltd for song and score 'One More Step', words and music Sydney Carter © 1971 Stainer & Bell Ltd; the author's agent (Roslyn Targ Literary Agency) for the story 'Me and Baby Brother' by Mary Stolz. Copyright © 1975 by Mary Stolz; Stanley Thornes Ltd for stories 'St. Cuthbert and the Eagle', 'St. Nicholas and the Bags of Gold', 'St. Paul' all by Jeanne L Jackson from *REDLETTER DAYS* 1995, poem 'Prayer' by Louise M. Haskins from *GATHERED TODAY* by Barbara Prosser, 1984; Wayland Publishers Ltd. for complete story 'The Story of the Minotaur' by John Snelling from *GREEK MYTHS AND LEGENDS*, 1987.

We have been unable to trace the copyright holders of the stories 'The Trouble with Ben' by Derek Farmer, 'Obtala, Creator of the Earth' by Penelope Farmer, 'Frederick' by Leo Lionni, 'The Easter Tree' by Richard Pinner, 'The Story of Light' by Susan Roth, 'The Story of the Last Supper' by Sue Spooner, 'Crab's Kingdom' by Tessa Suzuki-Morris, story 'Scott of the Antarctic' from *HEROES OF POLAR EXPEDITION* by Ralph & Andrist, stories 'The Willow Pattern', 'Noah's Ark', poems 'First Primrose' by Leonard Clark, 'Easter' by John Rice and poem 'A Place in the Sun', songs 'The Dingle-Dangle Scarecrow', 'Oats, Peas, Beans and Barley Grow', and would appreciate any information which would enable us to do so.

Addison Wesley Longman Limited.
Edinburgh Gate, Harlow, Essex, CM20 2JE, England
and Associated Companies throughout the world.

First published 1997
Second impression 1998
ISBN 0 582 30255 2

Produced by Addison Wesley Longman China Limited, Hong Kong.
EPC/02

The publisher's policy is to use paper manufactured from sustainable forests.

Contents

Active Assemblies

A cross-curricular approach to spiritual, moral, social and cultural education

In compiling *Active Assemblies Through the Year* I have taken account of current statutory requirements and OFSTED criteria, and based suggestions for delivery on sound educational principles intended to reflect good primary school practice.

Active Assemblies provides a multi-faceted resource bank which enables teachers to incorporate school assembly into their long-term planning, accommodate the 'one-off' in response to a significant event, or cater for those unexpected occasions when expedience rules.

Long-term curricular planning builds continuity and progression, avoids repetition and requires the involvement of the whole staff. Many primary schools favour the thematic approach and will find the opportunities for cross-curricular activity very useful in developing and extending classroom projects.

If, as has been suggested, '*school is the only structured, conceptualised form for a child's development into reponsible adulthood*', its ethos assumes even greater significance. The corporate nature of assembly provides an ideal opportunity to reaffirm the values at the heart of this ethos – values which are important to every member of the school 'family'. *Active Assemblies* contains a rich variety of stimuli with which to address PSE issues, celebrate high achievement, build a sense of fellowship, foster community links and citizenship, provide moments of awe and wonder, develop multicultural awareness and experience shared emotion and periods of reflection.

This emphasis on the school community and its responsibilities can be extended to embrace the immediate locality and, hence, society at large. The book contains resources relating to reponsibility for the environment, and demonstrates ways in which links with support agencies, multi-faith groups, ethnic communities etc can promote the 'one society' ideal at the heart of citizenship education.

As a headteacher with over 18 years practical experience in delivering school assemblies, however, I am only too aware that the best-laid plans can often come to grief in the busy, unpredictable world of primary education. The useful assembly book is one which can successfully accommodate the multifarious demands made upon the over-burdened teacher. It has been my prime objective to ensure that these practical needs are met, and thus, hopefully, prevent the book remaining on the shelf in the Head's office alongside countless other worthy, but ultimately less than useful publications.

Ian Addis

Chapter 1

Beginnings

*This is the beginning of a new day
God has given me this day to use as I will.
I can waste it or use it for good.
What I do today is important because I am
exchanging a day of my life for it.
When tomorrow comes this day will be gone
forever, leaving something I have traded for it.
I want it to be gain, not loss, good, not evil,
success, not failure, in order that I shall not
regret the price I paid for it.*

Anon

The start of a new school year is an ideal time to explore a number of topics within the central theme of 'Beginnings'.

Origins of the major world faiths

As there will be many references to the major world faiths throughout the book, it is appropriate to examine their origins here.

Christians follow the teachings and example of Jesus Christ, a Jew from Judaea, who lived about 2,000 years ago. Many believe Him to be the Son of God, and subscribe to the Nicene creed, dating from the fourth century.

> *We believe in one God the Father all Sovereign,*
> *maker of heaven and earth and of all things visible*
> *and invisible;*
>
> *And in one Lord Jesus Christ, the only begotten Son*
> *of God ...*
>
> *And in the Holy Spirit, the Lord and the life-giver,*
> *that proceeds from the Father and with the Father*
> *and Son is worshipped together and glorified*
> *together ...*

The 'father' of **Judaism** was Abraham, who lived in the Middle East about 4,000 years ago. He responded to a message from God, the creator of the world, to take his family to start a new life in a new place with new ideas. His people became the Hebrews. Jews, Muslims and Christians trace their ancestry back to Abraham (Ibrahim).

Muslims regard Adam, the first man, as the first of a number of prophets sent by Allah (God) to instruct mankind in caring for the world He had created, and in how to worship Him as the one true God. Ibrahim founded Islam in Makkah, birthplace of the last and greatest prophet, Muhammad.

Hinduism originated in northern India and is probably the oldest of the major world religions. Its followers believe in one supreme spirit known as Brahman, who has no form and is everywhere. The gods Brahma, Vishnu and Shiva are all parts of Brahman, and each has a function to perform:

Brahma, the creator of the world, is the *Generator*;
Vishnu, the preserver of life, is the *Organiser*;
Shiva, whose energy is both creative and destructive, is the *Destroyer*.

The **Sikh** religion was founded by Guru Nanak in the sixteenth century. It has its origins in Hinduism but differs in its belief in one God, the creator of all humanity. This is expressed in the opening words of the Sikh holy book, the Guru Granth Sahib.

> *There is one, and only one God,*
> *Whose name is Truth.*
> *God the Creator is without fear, without hate, immortal,*
> *Without form, and is beyond birth and death,*
> *And is understood through God's grace.*

The founder of **Buddhism** was an Indian prince, Siddhartha, who was born over 2,500 years ago. Siddhartha left a life of luxury and privilege to search for the cause and cure of suffering. Followers of Siddhartha, or Buddha (the awakened one), seek to emulate his Noble Eightfold Path to Enlightenment.

ADDITIONAL RESOURCES:

World Religions Series, Wayland
Living religions resource books and poster packs, Nelson
Religious Education Topics for the Primary School, John Rankin, Alan Brown and Mary Hayward, Longman
Religions of the World, Elizabeth Breuilly and Martin Palmer, Sainsbury's/Collins
A Gift to the Child: Religious Education in the Primary School, Simon and Schuster
Eye Witness Guides: Religion, Myrtle Langley, Dorling Kindersley
Infant Projects 111, Multi-Faith Topic, Child Education, Scholastic Publications

The Creation

Almost every culture has its own version of the origin of the world. Some are similar to the creation story from Genesis, others are vastly different, but all share a common attempt to explain man's predicament and his sense of wonder at natural phenomena.
This section contains a variety of creation stories from around the world.

Genesis

The first day

In the beginning God created the heavens and the earth. The earth was without form and empty. Darkness was everywhere and in the darkness the spirit of God moved upon the face of the deep.

God said: 'Let there be light,' and there was light.

God saw that it was good and he separated the light from the darkness. God called the light Day and the darkness he called Night.

And there were evening and morning: the first day.

The second day

God said: 'Let there be a sky in the midst of the waters and let it divide the waters from the waters.' Then God made the sky and he separated the waters above from the waters below.

God called the sky Heaven. And there were evening and morning: the second day.

The third day

God said: 'Let the waters under the heaven be gathered together in one place, and let the dry land appear.' And it was so. God called the dry land Earth, and the waters he called Seas. And he said:

'Let the earth bring forth grass, and yield plants bearing seed, and trees bearing fruit.' The earth did so and God saw that it was good.

This was the third day.

The fourth day

God said: 'Let there be lights in the sky of heaven to divide the day from the night. Let them be for signs and for seasons, for day from the night. Let them be for signs and for seasons, for days and for years. Let them be for lights in the sky of heaven to give light upon the earth.'

And it was so.

God made two great lights, the greater light to rule the day, and the lesser light to rule the night. He also made the stars and set them in the sky of heaven to give light upon the earth, to rule over the day and over the night, and to divide the light from the darkness. God saw that it was good.

This was the fourth day.

The fifth day

God said: 'Let the waters bring forth in great numbers moving creatures that have life, and let birds fly above the earth in the open sky of heaven.'

So God created great whales, and every living creature that moves. These the waters brought forth in great numbers. He created the birds, and saw that all this was good.

He blessed the creatures and said: 'Be fruitful and multiply, and fill the waters in the seas. Let the birds also multiply on earth.'

This was the fifth day.

The sixth day

God said: 'Let the earth bring forth creatures of all kinds, cattle and creeping things and beasts of the earth.' The earth did so and God saw that this was good.

'Let us make man in our image, after our likeness, and let him have power over the fish of the sea and the birds of the air, over the cattle, over all the earth and over everything that moves on the earth.'

So God created man in his own image. In the image of God he created man and woman. Male and female created he them. And he blessed them and said to them: 'Be fruitful and multiply. Fill the earth and have power over the fish of the sea and over the birds of the air, over every living thing that moves upon the earth.

'Behold, I have given you every plant bearing seed and every tree yielding fruit which is upon the face of the earth. They shall be your food. To every beast of the earth, to every bird of the air, to everything that creeps upon the earth and has life, I have given the grass and the plants for food.' And it was so. God saw everything that he had made, and it was very good. This was the sixth day.

The seventh day

The heavens and the earth were finished and filled with life. On the seventh day God rested from his work and all that he had made. God blessed the seventh day and made it a holy day, because on that day he had rested.

This is how the Lord God made the earth and the heavens, and every plant before it was in the earth, and every tree of the field before it grew. And when God had made man, a mist had gone up from the earth, and had watered the whole surface of the ground. The Lord God had formed man of the dust of the ground, and had breathed into him the breath of life, and man had become a living soul.

(A beautifully illustrated version of the above story can be found in The Story of the Creation *by Jane Ray, Letterbox Library.)*

Yhi, Mother of the Earth

Baiame, the great spirit and master of the universe, woke Yhi gently from her deep sleep.

'Come,' he whispered, his soft, soothing voice invading her dreams.

'You have slept long enough.'

Yhi stirred, stretched her arms, and wiped the sleep of centuries from her eyes.

Instantly, the dark land was bathed in warmth and light, and Baiame knew the long awaited moment was nigh.

'Go,' he said kindly. 'Carry your blessings to my chosen world.'

Yhi journeyed swiftly through the vast emptiness of space until she approached the giant ball that the great spirit called the Earth. As she gazed down, nothing moved across its barren, lifeless wastes. She felt no breath of wind, heard only an eerie silence. Yhi paused until she heard her master's voice once more.

'Do not hesitate, Yhi,' he said. 'Step down, step down.'

As her feet touched the sterile land, light beamed from her eyes, penetrating the inky blackness, and her kindly smile warmed the air, bringing life to the waiting world. Wherever she trod, flowers suddenly sprang up, released from their prisons deep in the earth, trees blossomed, shrubs emerged and grasses carpeted the ground between her toes.

But Baiame knew that the work was not yet done.

9

Hidden deep in the mighty snow-capped mountains were caves, carved in ice, each with their own secret.

'Carry your light into their coldest corners, Yhi,' he urged.

As she ventured deeper into the frozen heart of the mountains, Yhi stared defiantly at the pillars of glistening ice towering above her, mocking her puny frame. And when she felt the first slow drops of water on her upturned face she knew that she had won. Soon the slabs of melting ice were tumbling from the walls. Water splashed around her feet and trickled towards the mouth of the cave. The trickle became a stream, the stream became a torrent. As warmth wafted around inside the mountain, fish and reptiles and creatures of the deep, long entombed in frozen underground lakes, swam joyously in search of freedom.

Yet still Baiame knew that the work was not yet done.

'Do not stop Yhi,' he ordered. 'Find the great cavern!'

Obediently Yhi pressed onwards until she came to a huge chamber. Here, huddled together, a mass of fur and feather, were animals and birds of every kind. They crowded round their visitor, following her eagerly towards the light.

When Baiame saw Yhi at the head of the curious procession he at last smiled down upon the Earth.

'It is good,' he said, contentedly. 'The moment is truly come. My world is alive.'

(An Aboriginal story)

Obtala, Creator of the Earth

In his kingdom in the sky, high above the watery wasteland we now call the Earth, lived Olodumare, the most powerful god of the universe. All the other gods had to do his bidding, even Obtala, bravest and cleverest of his followers.

One day, Olodumare summoned Obtala and pointed down to the mass of marsh and swamp far below. Obtala had visited the wetland many times before with his friends, swinging across it on spiders' webs, for there was no solid earth on which to stand.

Nothing lived in the wetland.

No man.

No bird.

No beast.

It was a lifeless place.

'I want you, Obtala, to create the Earth,' the supreme god commanded.

'Take with you this snail shell filled with loose soil, some pieces of iron, a cockerel, a pigeon and a hen with five toes. Now, go and do my will!'

Eager to impress his master, Obtala swung from the spider's web as he had done so often before in play. But this was work and he had thought of a really clever plan. Hovering high above the marshland, he first threw down the iron bars and scattered them with soil from the snail shell. Then he carefully dropped the cockerel, the pigeon and the hen with five toes on to the tiny heaps of earth. It was in their nature to scratch, and scratch they did. And scratch and scratch and scratch and scratch, until little by little, grain by grain, the soil was spread further and further, until it had formed a large patch of solid earth.

Then Obtala stood upon the firm ground and waved to Olodumare in his kingdom in the sky.

Olodumare was so pleased with Obtala's work, that he allowed several of his friends to join him, building homes on the new earth. Our earth, created by Obtala. And a cockerel, a pigeon and a five toed hen.

(A Yoruba tale from Africa)

ADDITIONAL RESOURCES:

In the Beginning, Virginia Hamilton, Letterbox Library
Baby Earth, Michele Petit-Jean, Letterbox Library
Creation Stories, John Mayled, Wayland 1987
Myths and Legends from the World's Religions, John Bailey, OUP
Worlds of Difference, Martin Palmer, Esther Bisset, Blackie /WWF
In the Beginning, Kenneth McLeish, Longman
Junior Focus No 108, December 1996 (Scholastic Publications) contains valuable suggestions for a cross-curricular Creation Topic, including a comprehensive list of resources and useful addresses. (Single copies available from Subscriptions Dept., Scholastic Ltd., Westfield Road, Southam, Leamington Spa CV33 OJH).

Religious celebrations of birth

Some **Christians** celebrate the birth of a new baby through a church ceremony of baptism or 'christening'. The parents present their child in a public act of commitment, in which they promise to provide a Christian upbringing for the baby. The priest or minister administers the act of baptism, immersing the child in water, or pouring water over the child's forehead, sometimes marking the sign of the cross, as he speaks the words,

> *I baptise you in the name of the Father, and of the*
> *Son, and of the Holy Spirit. Amen.*

The child is now deemed to 'belong to Christ' and is part of the Christian community.

Jewish parents take their baby to the synagogue to welcome the child into the community. Boys will already have been initiated into the faith when only eight days old, as fathers fulfil the commandment in the Jewish holy book (the Torah) to have their sons circumcised. This is a demonstration that they have entered the covenant, or promise, of Abraham. The ritual is accompanied by the words,

> Just as he has entered into the covenant, so may he also enter into blessings of Torah, of marriage and of good deeds.

Muslims regard the birth of a baby as a gift from Allah (God). The first words heard by the new-born child should be from the Muslim call to prayer (the Adhan),

> Allah is most great
> Allah is most great
> I testify there is no god but Allah.

These words are whispered into the child's right ear. The words of the call to stand up for prayer (the Iqamah), are then spoken into the baby's left ear. This ritual is repeated at a gathering of family and friends, when the baby is about a week old, to celebrate his or her naming. Honey may be placed on the child's tongue, symbolising the taste of sweet words, and hair shaved from the head. Within certain Islamic cultures, the hair is then weighed, and a gift to the value of an equivalent weight of gold/silver is donated to charity.

Hindus may seek to ensure the welfare of the unborn child by performing a ceremony towards the end of the mother's pregnancy, when the family gather to recite prayers for a healthy child. On the day of the child's birth, and in the presence of a Hindu priest, the father takes a gold ornament dipped in clarified butter and honey (ghee) and holds it to the baby's lips. The words,

> May your life be as precious as gold. This will depend on your good thoughts, speech, deeds and behaviour.

are recited by the father or the priest, who then whispers into the baby's right ear,

> May God the creator of all things grant you firm wisdom. Knowledge and wisdom are the source of power and long life.

Sikh families also welcome the arrival of a new baby as a gift from God. A ceremony is held, either at the gurdwara (temple), or at the family home, when the birth is celebrated in words from the Sikh holy book (the Guru Granth Sahib). For example,

> The true Lord has sent the child. The long-lived child has been born by good fortune. The Sikhs sing God's praises in their joy.

At the end of the service the holy book is opened at random and a

Shabad (hymn) is chosen, the initial letter of which will provide the first letter of the baby's name. When the family have made their decision the name is announced to the congregation.

Buddhist parents take their baby to the monastery where they can request a special name for the child. Holy water is flicked over the new baby and its family at a ceremony in which the monks and nuns offer blessings – for its future welfare, happiness and noble qualities.

Birth

Head first, purple like a prune,
unplugged from spongy silence
I cringe at the sting of brightness

The journey's over
Slapped into anger I learn language
thump fists, kick.

The journey begins.

Gina Dowthwaite

Me and the baby brother

The arrival of a baby brother or sister into the family brings excitement, but it can also create its own tensions. These are beautifully expressed in this story by Mary Stolz.

First thing in the morning Dad said to me, 'Guess what? You have a baby brother now.'

I said, 'I don't want a baby brother.'

He said, 'Well, you've already got him. Isn't that great?'

I said, 'Where is he?'

Dad said, 'At the hospital – with your mother.'

I said, 'Mum can come home and leave him at the hospital. That'll be okay.'

Dad said, 'That's no way to talk.'

So I stopped talking.

After a while Dad said, 'We are going to let you help name your baby brother. I would like to name him Tom, and your mother thinks Bill would be a good name. What do you think?'

I thought. Then I said, 'Let's name him Dustbin.'

Dad said. 'You are being very difficult.'

I said, 'Dustbin is a good name. Nobody else will be named Dustbin. Practically everybody is named Bill or Tom. Dustbin. That's a good name for him.'

Dad said, 'I think we'll do without your help.'

I said, 'That's okay with me. I don't care what you name him anyway. Hey, how about that? You could call him Anyway.'

Dad said, 'He's part of our family now. I expect you'll get to like him.'

I didn't say anything.

Then my aunt came to take me to a birthday party I got invited to before they sprung the baby brother on me.

She said, 'Isn't it wonderful that you have a baby brother?'

I said. 'Ugh!'

She smiled. 'Oh my, I'd like to be there when he comes home. What will you do when you first seem him?'

'Hit him.'

Dad and Aunty looked at each other, and they looked at the ceiling. Aunty said, 'You'd better get dressed, dear.'

So I got dressed to go to this yucky birthday party. I used to like birthday parties, but not any more. This one was awful. First they all got mad at me when I put mustard and salt and pepper on my piece of birthday cake.

'Why are you doing that?' my aunt asked loudly. She frowned.

I said, 'It's too sweet.'

Aunty said, 'Oh, I'm so sorry.' Only she didn't say it to me, but to the yucky kid's mother who made the gooey cake. Even with the mustard and salt and pepper it was too sweet.

Then this kid pulled the cat's tail. So I knocked him down and said, 'Be gentle!' Why did they all get mad at that? You're supposed to be gentle with animals.

Then I tried to take one of the presents away from the yucky kid, and he yelled like a baboon. I said, 'Share! Didn't anybody teach you you're supposed to share?'

They took the present away from me and gave it back to him. After the way they always tell me I have to share.

Aunty said I was spoiling the party and took me home. Boy, I didn't care one bit.

Dad came home early from work, and we made dinner together. We had chicken and rice and green beans, and for pudding he made chocolate sundaes.

I said 'You're as good a cooker as Mum.'

He said, 'As good a cook, not cooker.'

Cook. Cooker. Who cares? I was trying to make a compliment. I don't think people should correct other people's compliments.

I said, 'You know what I'm going to be when I grow up?'

'What?'

'A bird.'

'A bird?'

'A bird without any children.'

He said, 'Why do you want to be a bird?'

But he didn't ask why no children.

I said, 'So I can fly away.'

'From here?'

'Yes, from here.'

He said, 'You'd fly away from us, too?'

I said, 'I'd fly away so far, I'd fly away from me.'

'I see.' He sounded kind of sad.

'Well, I'd fly back. Probably.'

'That's a relief.'

After a while he said, 'Do you want to go to the hospital to see your mother?'

I said, 'Sure.' I waited for him to say something about the baby brother, but he didn't.

When we got to the hospital he said, 'If you want to wait in that room, I'll walk down the hall and look through the glass at – at the new baby.'

I said, 'I might as well come along.'

The nurse held up the baby brother for us to look at. Boy, is he ugly. I said, 'We'd better not call him Dustbin.'

Dad said, 'I'm glad you've changed your mind.'

I said, 'With looks like that, he needs a lot of help. Maybe you can call him Thomas William. Or William Thomas.'

Dad laughed. 'Maybe he'll get better looking in time.'

I said, 'I sure hope so.'

ADDITIONAL RESOURCES:

Henry's Baby, Mary Hoffman, Dorling Kindersley
Billie and Belle, Sarah Garland, Letterbox Library
Will There Be a Lap for Me?, Dorothy Carey, Letterbox Library
Welcoming Babies, Margy Burns-Knight, Letterbox Library

Return to school

At the beginning of the new school year, school assembly plays an important role by integrating new arrivals into the community and reaffirming the school ethos. The emphasis is often upon the 'Family of school', rights and responsibilities of membership, and explanations of the rules which safeguard members' welfare. For a school community to thrive, as in the world outside, everyone must be prepared to contribute a little to get something in return.

Prayer for our school

This is our school
Let peace dwell here
Let the rooms be full of contentment
Let love abide here
Love of mankind
Love of life itself
And love of God.
Let us remember
That, as many hands build a house
So many hearts make a school.

Words traditional, music by Ralph E. Pearce

Melanie Brown and the new class

Sometimes moving into a new class can cause problems.

One day Mrs Collins called six of the children together and told them that because they were so clever they could soon go up into the next class with Mrs Jones. Melanie Brown was one of the six and she listened carefully to what Mrs Collins had to say. Then she thought the matter over and decided against it.

'Because I like it best in this class,' she said. Christopher stared at her in horror.

'But I'm going,' he said. 'What will you do without me?'

Melanie Brown didn't know and she didn't care.

'I don't like Mrs Jones,' she said. 'She's not pretty – and she's a bit old.'

'She's not old,' said Denise, 'and she's ever so kind – and you do hard sums in her class.'

'That's true,' said Mrs Collins quickly. 'The work in this class is very easy really and you six are clever enough to do more grown-up work.'

'I like easy work,' said Melanie Brown firmly, and she went back to her table to finish her painting. Christopher's big blue eyes filled with tears as he looked at Mrs Collins.

'If Melanie's not going then I don't want to go,' he said shakily.

'Nor do I', said Paula.

John and Susan didn't say anything but they didn't look very happy. Mrs Collins sighed.

'Well,' she said, 'Go back to what you were doing and we'll talk about it another day.'

'When I've sorted out Melanie Brown,' she added to herself and wondered how to go about it.

Melanie Brown was very pleased with her painting. It was a picture of a garden. She had put hundreds and hundreds of blades of grass at the bottom of the picture and big splodgy roses up each side. The middle was fully of navy blue flowers. 'Primroses,' she told Paula, who looked rather surprised. She decided to add a big yellow sun and dipped her brush into the yellow paint. She drew a big round circle – and then gave a sudden roar of rage that shocked the whole class into silence.

'Melanie!' cried Mrs Collins. 'Whatever is the matter?'

'My picture!' shrieked Melanie Brown. 'It's all gone horrible! The sun's all green!'

They all crowded round and sure enough the sun was green. Not very green, it's true, but a nasty yellowy green, not a bit like the sun. Melanie Brown glared fiercely around, then pointed accusingly at the jar of yellow paint.

'Someone's mixed the colours,' she said. 'Someone's put the blue brush in the yellow.'

'Poor Melanie,' said Mrs Collins. 'What a shame. It was such a nice picture, too. Still, I'm sure it was an accident.'

'It was Michael,' said Denise. 'I saw him.'

Melanie Brown gave Michael a horrid look, snatched her painting from the easel and screwed it up. She threw it on to the floor and started to cry. Christopher tried to cheer her up but in the end she had to sit on Mrs Collins's lap for a few minutes with a handful of Dolly Mixtures.

'Don't be cross with Michael,' said Mrs Collins. 'He is only five and he hasn't been at school long. He doesn't know about paints yet.'

Melanie Brown said nothing, but she sniffed very loudly several times and put five Dolly Mixtures into her mouth at once.

Mrs Collins gave her a paper tissue to wipe her eyes with and suggested that she start another picture, but Melanie Brown had gone off the idea of painting and decided to read a book instead.

In the afternoon Mrs Collins asked Melanie Brown to take a note to Mrs Jones, and that pleased her, because she loved doing important things. She marched round to Mrs Jones's room and knocked on the door. The children called out, 'Come in,' so she did. She gave Mrs Jones the note and waited while she read it in case there was going to be an answer.

'Mrs Collins wants to borrow some books,' said Mrs Jones.

'While I'm finding them perhaps you would like to have a look round and see what the children are doing.'

So Melanie Brown began a tour of the room. In one corner she found some children mixing cake-mixture in a big bowl.

'We're making cakes,' they told her proudly. 'The cook is going to bake them in her big oven for us.'

In the Book Corner two boys were reading about aeroplanes and writing things down in their books. But it was the painting that interested Melanie Brown most. To her surprise there were no pots of paint like the ones they used in her own class. Instead the children had a small tray each. Six plastic pots fitted into each tray and these were filled with different-coloured powders.

'It's powder paint,' one of the boys told her kindly. 'We mix our own colours in this class. Look, I'll show you.'

He stirred some yellow and some red paint together and added a little water.

'There you are! Orange!'

Melanie Brown was enchanted.

'I know about mixing colours,' she said. 'I'll mix you some green.'

And before he could say, 'No, thank you,' she had taken the brush and was mixing blue and yellow powder to make green.

'There you are,' she said proudly. 'Now you can have some grass in the picture.'

The boy was just explaining that it was a picture of a jet plane flying in the sky and he didn't need any grass, and Melanie Brown was telling him that a jet plane landing on some grass would be a much better picture, when Mrs Jones interrupted them.

'Here you are, Melanie,' she said. 'These are the books Mrs Collins wants to borrow and thank you for bringing the message.'

Reluctantly Melanie Brown went back to her own room. She put the books on Mrs Collins's desk without a word and stood deep in thought, scuffing the toe of one shoe along the floor. The teacher watched her hopefully. At last Melanie Brown gave a little sigh and looked up.

'I think I will go into Mrs Jones's class after all,' she said. 'She's not as old as I thought – and she is a bit pretty.'

Mrs Collins smiled broadly and said she thought Melanie Brown had made a very wise decision.

Pamela Oldfield

ADDITIONAL RESOURCES:

Sometimes I Don't Like School, Paula Hogan, Blackwell Raintree
Stew from The Mouse that Roared, Ray Jones, Heinemann

Log book extracts

It is often interesting to identify changes in the way schools function, by examining records and artefacts from the past. One of the most useful is the school log book, which can provide valuable insight into school life in former times.

May 1st 1850

'On the first anniversary of the school, 150 children walked to Boughton House with flags and banners. From there they moved to the Parish Church where a sermon was preached ... Tea was served in the schoolroom presided over by Their Graces, The Duke and Duchess of Buccleuch.'

October 1890 Report by Her Majesty's Inspector after annual inspection

'The children are well behaved, their work has considerably improved, and they passed a good examination, both in elementary and class subjects. More problems might be worked in arithmetic. The boys have a creditable knowledge of geography, but it was a little too mechanical in Standards One and Two. Singing was good. The garments might be in a more finished state, and the First Standard should show a chain edge in knitting; but otherwise the needlework has been nicely taught.'

('Wherefore art thou OFSTED?')

April 16th 1915

'The attendance has been lower today, especially this afternoon, owing to the visit of a circus to Kettering.'

September 27th–October 18th

'10 half-holidays allowed for blackberrying.'

February 10th 1924

'Opened school this morning with thermometer at 30. Ink all frozen solid.'

December 12th 1924

'I have been compelled to unite five standards – 73 children into one class for three weeks.'

May 10th 1933

'Shaft of hoe accidentally broken in school garden. It will be useful for small boy in present state.'

September 30th 1940

'210 children now in school – 132 natives, 78 evacuees.'

March 6th 1947

'Heavy blizzards and deep drifts of snow. Fires banked all night.'

March 10th 1947

'Thawing – Classroom 2 is flooded – the water comes up through the floorboards.'

February 15th 1952

'The children worked quietly in the wireless room listening to the broadcast description of the late King George V1's funeral.'

(Geddington CE Primary School, Northamptonshire)

Activities

Dramatisation of stories

The Creation myths, retold on page (7 – 11), can easily be adapted for use in assembly. See *Elleni and the Sharing Bread* (page 44).

Baby photographs

A display of baby photographs could be constructed and linked to a 'Growth' project, incorporating the care and welfare of babies and including input from parents, the school nurse and a health visitor.

Rules for our class

Be kind to other people.

Be safe and sensible.

We only need these two rules because they mean all those don'ts like don't shout out, don't hurt, don't criticise cruelly, don't stand on your chair, don't talk at the wrong time, don't push and don't waste time.

Jennifer

Naming ceremonies

Investigations into naming ceremonies could involve the collection and display of artefacts, visits to places of worship, and input from representatives with multi-faith backgrounds.

Devising class rules

Individual classes could draw up lists of rules to govern acceptable behaviour in the classroom. This could be extended to include other areas of school, e.g. cloakrooms, corridors, the playground. Reasons for the inclusion of specific rules could be discussed, leading to wider debate amongst class representatives and subsequent adoption by the whole school community.

This is our class

Welcome posters displayed in a prominent position in the classroom apply to visitors and class members alike.

Children can be given a sense of identity in their new class through compiling individual profiles containing self-portraits, pen pictures, 'vital' statistics, details about homes, family backgrounds, hobbies and interests etc. Information amassed can be collated, to provide an overview of the class as a whole.

Ourselves topic

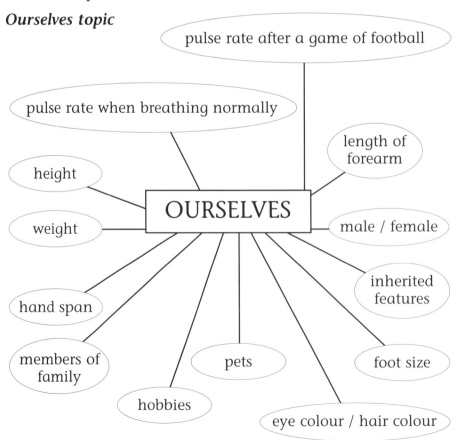

ADDITIONAL RESOURCES:

Your Health: Health and Drugs, D Baldwin, Wayland

Devising plans of the classroom

This activity develops mapping skills but also heightens children's awareness of the location of resources and increases their sense of ownership of and responsibility for them.

This is our school

Once again, the strategic use of welcome posters, designed by pupils, can make an immediate impression on visitors. The integration process can be enhanced by individual classes contributing to a large display which features a plan of the school building and identifies the location of classes, members of staff and the differing functions of areas of the school site etc. Younger children might undertake guided journeys around the school, to familiarise them with its geography.

Children can investigate the varied contributions made by members of the school personnel by devising questionnaires, interviewing staff, producing sketches and sharing results with the rest of the school in assembly.

This was our school

Examination of the school log book might lead to the collation and display of records, photographs, newspaper cuttings etc. featuring important events in the school's history.

Newsletters

One practical method of disseminating information about the school and its activities is for children to produce newsletters, the contents of which can be shared during assembly, displayed, and distributed around the building.

Chapter 2

One of the Team

A stained-glass window commemorating the life of Duncan Edwards, footballer

So many activities today, both in school and in the wider world, involve teamwork. At a time in the school year when many children are striving for a place in representative sides, it is opportune to consider the responsibilities of team membership, the integration of individual skills, and the co-operation and collaboration that any group activity requires.

Choosing the team

A graphic demonstration of the importance of unifying individual skills and attributes can be provided by the tangram, or teamgram. The seven apparently disparate sections of the tangram, representing the seven members of a netball team, can only fit together and 'gel' when arranged in a special way. A mismatch, where individual pieces are placed haphazardly or at random, fails to achieve any recognisable or effective pattern.

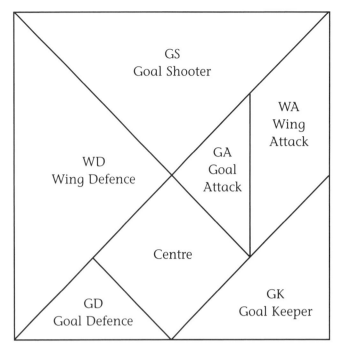

Major world faiths

Jesus Christ spent the final three years of his life teaching about the Kingdom of God. He gathered a team of twelve people, known as disciples, who travelled with him and were his companions in his work. (Mark 3:14–19)

A modern interpretation, using football as a metaphor, sees the disciples as members of Jesus's 'team'. An assembly can be introduced by the *Match of the Day* tune, each 'player' described separately on an OHP, with their individual qualities listed. The 'manager' can be described at the end.

This can lead to discussion with the children regarding their perceptions of good 'team-play' etc.

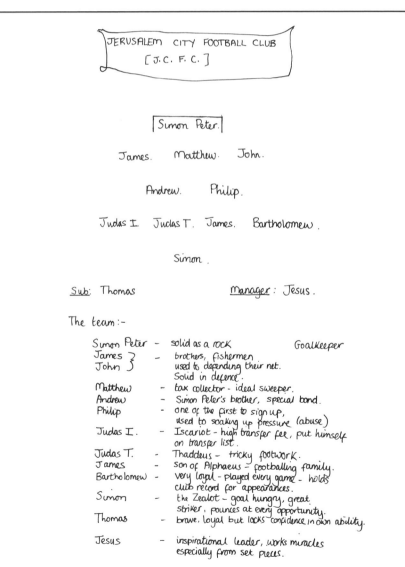

Moses is regarded by **Jews** as their leading teacher. After rescuing his people from captivity in Egypt, 3,200 years ago, Moses received the Torah, the rules for life, from God on Mount Sinai. By the first century CE, the Jews were dispersed throughout the Middle East and Europe and had created synagogues wherever they settled. The Torah became increasingly important and rabbis, wise or learned people who could interpret its contents, spread the word among their communities.

Muslims believe that as the teachings of Ibrahim (Abraham), the first prophet, were forgotten, Allah sent more, culminating in Muhammad, the final and greatest prophet. On receiving a message from the angel Jibril (Gabriel), to proclaim the word of God, Muhammad spent the next 23 years receiving revelations containing Allah's guidance (the Qur'an). After his death, his companion, Abu Bakr, was chosen by some to lead the community. His followers were known as Sunni ('people of the custom of the prophets') and they believed in the democratic election of the leader. Others supported Ali, Muhammad's cousin and son-in-law. They favoured hereditary succession and were called Shi'ah. The division remains to this day, although both sects use the Qur'an, follow the example of the prophet Muhammad, and share Islamic beliefs.

Hindu scriptures, or Shastras, are texts that explain and guide the way people behave in life. They have their origin in the 'heard' or 'revealed' scriptures (Shruti), which were presented by wise men in ancient times who are believed to have heard God's word directly. These scriptures were passed on orally for hundreds of years by gurus (teachers) before being written down. Many current Hindu practices date from the Puranic period (300–1200 CE), and two influential thinkers from that period were Shankara and Ramanuja.

Guru Nanak

This story demonstrates how the first Guru, Guru Nanak, brought God's message to the people.

It was morning and people had gone to wash and bathe in the river. They would pick up water in their hands and throw it towards the rising sun.

Nanak went down to the riverside and faced the other way with his back to the sun. He bent down, picked up some water in his hands and threw it in the 'wrong' direction.

The people were amazed. Was the stranger mad? They asked him,

'What do you think you are doing?'

'What do you think *you* are doing?' replied Nanak.

'We throw water towards the sun for the sake of our ancestors who have died. They have gone to live in the other world where the sun rises,' the people explained.

Nanak smiled, walked back to the river, and went on throwing water towards the west where the sun sets. Now the people began to grow really angry. Someone shouted,

'How dare you throw water in the wrong direction?'

'I live in the Punjab, west of here,' said Nanak. 'It's been very dry over there, so I'm sending some water to make my crops grow.'

They laughed at him.

'Your water won't reach the Punjab?' they said.

'Yours won't reach the sun either,' Nanak told them.

He then explained that what they were doing was useless. The sun was not made by people. It was something wonderful made by God. Instead of throwing water towards it, they would do much, much better to pray, work hard and help other people.

(Adapted from a traditional Sikh story)

Sikhs are initiated into the Khalsa (Sikh community) during a ceremony called 'Amrit' which commemorates the example of the Panj piare (Five Beloved Ones). At the new year festival of Baisakhi in 1699 CE, Guru Gobind Singh, the tenth and last human Guru, drew his sword and asked for one of the vast crowd to surrender his life for the faith. The first volunteer was taken into a nearby tent from which the Guru later emerged with his sword dripping blood. This was repeated four times before the Guru appeared again, with all five men still alive. He explained that this had been a test of their courage and willingness to die for their faith and the Guru.

Some years after **Prince Siddhartha** renounced his life of luxury for that of a wandering, homeless monk, he joined five ascetics (men who deliberately went without food and sleep). Almost dying of hunger, Siddhartha was forced to accept some rice. He was rejected by his five friends who thought him weak and soft. When his strength returned, he resolved to acquire true understanding through meditation. On achieving a state of perfect joy and peace, 'Nirvana', he began travelling through India, teaching about the nature of human existence and how people could be freed from their suffering. His first followers were the five ascetics who had once abandoned him. His family, too, accepted his teaching and a community known as the Sangha was formed by his aunt, who became the first **Buddhist** nun.

Famous sporting teams

Record books are filled with the achievements of great sporting teams. Many provide useful examples of individual talent, spirit, and collective endeavour.

The team that wouldn't die

In 1996, Manchester United became the first English football team to achieve an FA Cup and League double for the second time. Yet it is doubtful if manager Alex Ferguson will ever attain the special place in the affection of United fans reserved for the late Sir Matt Busby.

On 6 February 1958, Manchester United's team of young players, nicknamed the 'Busby Babes', were flying home after victory over Red Star Belgrade in the quarter-final of the European Cup. They were then, as now, the most successful club side in the country, having won the League Championship in the two previous seasons. The star-studded team included England captain Roger Byrne, fellow internationals Duncan Edwards and Tommy Taylor, and a promising young forward called Bobby Charlton.

The Manchester United party, and a host of accompanying newspapermen, had arrived at Munich airport, where the plane had refuelled. At three minutes past three on that wintry afternoon, after two unsuccessful attempts to take off in dreadful conditions, the British European Airways Flight 609 ZU taxied on to the runway, its wheels rolling through ice and slush. Once again the twin-engined Elizabethan airliner failed to leave the ground, but this time there was no safe return to the airport. The plane broke in half, before coming to rest, a heap of tangled wreckage strewn across the fields surrounding the airport.

Irish international goalkeeper Harry Gregg, who had escaped unscathed from the crash, ignored the risk of explosion to return to the stricken aircraft and rescue trapped passengers, including a tiny baby. Amongst the survivors he found manager Matt Busby, critically injured, and Bobby Charlton, lying in a pool of water.

First reports of the crash to reach England failed to present a true account of the disaster. The six o'clock news, however, revealed to a stunned television audience the true extent of the horror – seven Manchester United players were among the 21 passengers killed. Busby and Duncan Edwards were fighting for their lives.

Old Trafford became a shrine for the next home match on 19 February, when 59,848 spectators watched crash survivors, hero Harry Gregg and new captain Bill Foulkes, help a scratch United side to victory over Sheffield Wednesday.

The programme notes included this prophetic message:

'... The road back may be long and hard but with the memory of those who died at Munich, of their stirring achievements and wonderful sportsmanship ever with us ... MANCHESTER UNITED WILL RISE AGAIN.'

Sadly, Duncan Edwards, regarded by many as the greatest

player ever to wear the famous United jersey, died of his injuries two days later. He was just 21 years old. But, against all odds, Matt Busby recovered to build a team that would fulfil that unlikely promise. And just ten years later, Bill Foulkes and Bobby Charlton were among the Manchester United players who became the first English winners of the European Cup. Busby was knighted later in the summer of 1968, assured of his place in footballing history.

(A memorial stained-glass window in the parish church of his home town, Dudley, in Worcestershire, commemorates the life of Duncan Edwards. This is reproduced on page 24.)

Making use of our talents

Everyone is blessed with some skill or attribute which can be developed to the full. In the Parable of the Talents, Jesus reminds us of our responsibility to make the best use of our abilities.
(Matthew 25:14–29)

Frederick

It is not always easy to recognise the true worth of an individual, especially if that person is regarded as 'different' or an outsider.

All along the meadow where the cows grazed and the horses ran, there was an old stone wall.

In that wall, not far from the barn and the granary, a chatty family of field mice had their home.

But the farmer had moved away, the barn was abandoned, and the granary stood empty. And since winter was not far off, the little mice began to gather corn and nuts and wheat and straw. They all worked day and night. All – except Frederick.

'Frederick, why don't you work?' they asked.

'I do work,' said Frederick. 'I gather sun rays for the cold dark winter days.'

And when they saw Frederick sitting there, staring at the meadow, they said, 'And now, Frederick?' 'I gather colours,' answered Frederick simply. 'For winter is grey.'

And once Frederick seemed half asleep. 'Are you dreaming Frederick?' they asked reproachfully. But Frederick said, 'Oh no, I am gathering words. For the winter days are long and many, and we'll run out of things to say.'

And the winter days came, and when the first snow fell the five little field mice took to their hideout in the stones.

In the beginning there was lots to eat, and the mice told stories of foolish foxes and silly cats. They were a happy family.

But little by little they had nibbled up most of the nuts and berries, the straw was gone, and the corn was only a memory. It was cold in the wall and no one felt like chatting.

Then they remembered what Frederick had said about sun rays and colours and words. 'What about your supplies, Frederick?' they asked.

'Close your eyes,' said Frederick, as he climbed on a big stone. 'Now I send you the rays of the sun. Do you feel how their golden glow ...' And as Frederick spoke of the sun the four little mice began to feel warmer. Was it Frederick's voice? Was it magic?

'And how about the colours, Frederick?' they asked anxiously. 'Close your eyes again,' Frederick said. And when he told them of the blue periwinkles, the red poppies in the yellow wheat, and the green leaves of the berry bush, they saw the colours as clearly as if they had been painted in their minds.

'And the words, Frederick?'

Frederick cleared his throat, waited a moment, and then, as if from a stage, he said:

'Who scatters the snowflakes? Who melts the ice?
Who spoils the weather? Who makes it nice?
Who grows the four-leaf clovers in June?
Who dims the daylight? Who lights the moon?

Four little field mice who live in the sky.
Four little field mice ... like you and I.
One is the Springmouse who turns on the shower.
Then comes the Summer who paints in the flower.
The Fallmouse is next with walnuts and wheat.
And Winter is last ... with little cold feet.

Aren't we lucky the seasons are four?
Think of a year with one less ... or one more!'

When Frederick had finished, they all applauded. 'But Frederick,' they said, 'you are a poet!'

Frederick blushed, took a bow, and said shyly, 'I know it.'

Leo Lionni

The trouble with Ben

Newcomers can sometimes experience difficulty in gaining acceptance by the class or school community and there appears to be no place in the team.

The trouble with Ben was he was different from the rest of the class. For a start – he looked different. Tall and gangly, with tightly curled hair and bright blue eyes. Then again, he sounded different. Spoke in a different way, with a different accent.

See, Ben's family hadn't long moved into the area. He was a newcomer, in a place where newcomers weren't always welcome.

Not unless they fitted in easily, like Simon Billingham. He was a newcomer as well. In fact he'd started at school later than Ben had. But Simon fitted in. For a start, he was noisy. Always laughing and making jokes and thinking up nicknames for people. But more than that, Simon Billingham was good at games. Football? He could play anywhere. Up front. In defence. Midfield. Even in goal. Cricket, rounders, netball, he was always first to be picked. But Ben, he was always last. The one still standing against the wall when everybody else had been chosen.

'You can have Ben,' both Captains would say, trying to make sure he was on the other side. See, no matter how hard he tried, Ben would always be the one who scored an own goal. Or gave away a penalty. Or kicked his own side's best player by mistake. Or headed the ball over the railings into the road – where a bus would run over it and squash it flat.

In the end he was banned from playtime games. Not that he minded all that much. He knew he was no good. And really he'd rather sit on a bench and read a comic. Or work out a new program for the battered old computer that his big sister had passed down to him. That computer was what gave Simon Billingham the idea for Ben's nickname – 'Acorn'! Soon everybody was calling him that. Ben didn't bother; most of them said it in a friendly way. It even made Ben feel more like one of the team. Not so much of a newcomer.

That was the only way he was one of the team though. He was certainly never in the sports team. Because, whenever it came to games, Ben always volunteered to step in and tidy the library. Or clean out the guinea pigs. Or wash up the paint palettes. So when his teacher Mrs Brooklyn suggested a boys versus girls rounders match, Ben was the first to spot the problem.

'Please, Mrs Brooklyn,' he said. 'There's fourteen boys and only thirteen girls.'

'Yes, that's not fair,' all the girls yelled.

'Don't worry,' said Ben, 'I'll drop out. That'll make it thirteen a side.'

So that was what they agreed. Until the day of the big match came – and Kenny Jackson didn't.

'Kenny's got mumps,' Mrs Brooklyn told the class. 'Ben – you'll have to take his place to keep the sides even.'

The boys groaned. And the girls cheered. And Ben wished *he'd* got mumps.

'Just do your best, Ben,' Mrs Brooklyn smiled. 'After all, it's only a game.'

But to the rest of the class it was more than a game. It was a battle, boys versus girls.

The girls batted first and got three rounders. In reply, the boys knocked six. Even though Ben was out before he even got to first base. Then, in their second innings, the girls batted like demons. Round and round they kept going. Time after time. And finished up with a total of fifteen.

'That means that we'll have to get ten to win,' moaned Jamie Patterson. 'We'll never do it.'

'Oh yes we will,' said Simon Billingham, and knocked a rounder with his first hit. Now it was the boys' turn to do well. And they did do. Even Ben managed to avoid getting out, though he never hit the ball once.

But gradually, one by one, the girls ran them out. Till there were only two boys left in – Simon Billingham and Ben. Simon stepped up for his turn, smashed the ball the length of the field and raced round. That put the boys just one rounder behind the girls.

'Don't try and hit it. You just run,' Simon hissed at Ben. 'Leave me to knock the rounders.'

But Ben sensed his moment of glory had come. He picked up his bat and stepped forward. This time he was determined. For once in his life he was going to show everybody he could do it. He was going to hammer that ball out of sight. Wendy Patrick stepped up to bowl. Ben swung – and missed. His heart sank. He dropped the bat and started to run to first base. But before he got there Mrs Brooklyn's voice rang out. 'No ball! Have another go, Ben.'

Ben walked back to his place and got ready. Wendy bowled. Ben swung the bat, and clunk – he made contact. The ball went whizzing through the air. He'd done it! He'd hit the ball! Feeling ten feet tall, he started to run. The ball was still high in the air. Past first base. The ball still hadn't hit the ground. He could do it, he could get a rounder. Then up popped Shirley Jenkins, right under where the ball was falling. She didn't even have to move! Just keep her eyes on the ball. Put up her hands. And –

'Out!' shouted Mrs Brooklyn. 'Caught out. That means the innings is over. The girls have won by one rounder.'

Ben was dumbstruck. The only time he'd hit it, and he'd got the whole team out. The next thing he knew, he was being pushed and jostled by the other boys.

'You idiot, Acorn!' yelled Simon Billingham. 'If it hadn't been for you we would have won.'

And the worst thing was, Ben knew that it was true. Then and there he vowed he'd never *ever* be one of the team again. And he stuck to that vow. Until a few weeks later, when something happened to change his mind.

'Class six have challenged us to a chess match,' Mrs Brooklyn said. 'Their four best players against ours. Hands up those who can play chess.'

Five girls put their hands up and two boys, one of them Ben.

'Is that all?' said Mrs Brooklyn. 'Only two boys can play chess! Simon, what about you? Can't you play?'

'Yes of course I can,' Simon said. 'I can play any game.'

'That makes eight then,' said Mrs Brooklyn. 'We'll have a competition next Tuesday after school, the four winners of that will make up our team.'

Well, I suppose it was bound to happen really. Ben was picked to play against, yes, Simon Billingham.

The chess matches started at four o'clock. The classroom was empty except for the eight players and Mrs Brooklyn. But outside, trying to look in through the windows, was just about the whole of the rest of the class. Ben was playing the white pieces so it was his turn first. He took hold of a pawn and moved it forward two squares. Simon stared at the board, his fists were clenched so tightly his knuckles were turning white. A minute passed by, Ben wondered what he was waiting for. Then Simon looked up at him. But it was a different Simon. His face was pale and drawn. His eyes were staring. And his tongue licked nervously at his lips. He was in a panic. It was then Ben realised what was wrong. Simon Billingham didn't know how to play chess! He hadn't a clue how the pieces moved. For a few seconds the boys stared at each other. Then Ben hissed under his breath, 'Just do whatever I do. Make the same moves.'

Well – to cut a long story short – that's what Simon did. He followed every move that Ben made. And so the game went on until Ben decided it was enough and finished the match off.

Outside in the playground the boys crowded round.

'Jammy! That's what it was,' said Darren Baraclough.

'Yeh, just luck, wasn't it, Simon?' yelled Jamie Patterson.

'No', said Simon, 'it wasn't luck at all. He beat me easy. Ben's the best chess player I've ever played. He ought to be Captain of the chess team.'

'Yes – Ben for chess Captain!' shouted Jamie Patterson. And the boys charged off across the playground chanting, 'Ben for Captain, Ben for Captain,' as they went.

Ben and Simon were left alone. 'Why did you say you could play?' Ben asked.

'I didn't want everybody to know I couldn't. I'm supposed to be able to play everything. Anyway, my Dad said he'd teach me but then, well, he had to go away for a few days, so I was stuck.'

'I see.' Ben nodded.

'Anyway thanks,' said Simon, 'and I really did mean that about you being Captain at chess.'

'I don't want to be Captain,' said Ben. 'I just want a place in the team.'

Derek Farmer

Topiwalo the hat-maker

A true leader will often need to think around a problem, as in this traditional Indian folk-tale.

Once upon a time there was a hat-maker. He was a very old man and he lived in a wooden house in a small Indian village. He made his hats from the finest straw.

Every Friday he loaded some of his hats on to a little barrow and set off to sell them in a little village a few miles away. The children would gather to say goodbye to him calling TOPIWALO, TOPIWALO.

One Friday the sun was so hot, the old hat-maker had to sit down and rest. He found a shady spot under a tree. Very soon he was fast asleep. The old man was so tired that he had not noticed the playful monkeys climbing in the tree. They watched the hat-maker with great interest.

One monkey who was more adventurous than the others climbed down the tree and had a look inside the barrow. When he saw the hats, he picked one up and put it on his head. The other monkeys watched him for a minute then one by one, they climbed down and tried on all the hats in the barrow. The old man stayed fast asleep.

Suddenly the old man woke up. He glanced up into the tree and was very surprised to see the monkeys – and very cross when he discovered that each monkey was wearing one of his hats!

'Give me back my hats,' he shouted at the monkeys, and shook his fist at them. The monkeys shook their fists at the old man. The hat-maker glared at the monkeys – but they only glared back at him.

The old man took his hat off his head and scratched his forehead. He didn't know how to get his hats back. As he looked at the monkeys they took off their hats and scratched their foreheads. The hat-maker put his hat back on his head and watched the monkeys carefully. The monkeys put their hats back on their heads too.

'AH!' thought the old man. 'Now I know what to do.' He took off his hat and threw it onto the ground. Then he watched the monkeys to see what they would do.

The monkeys watched the hat-maker. Then they too took off their hats and threw them onto the ground. The old man smiled. 'Thank you,' he said. The monkeys looked back at him and began to chatter. The hat-maker began to pick up his hats and put them back into his barrow. 'Thank you very much my friends,' he said to the monkeys. Then he picked up the barrow and began walking slowly along the path to the village.

Elaine Abrahams

Activities

Dramatisation of stories

The Parable of the Talents, the story of Frederick, 'A place in the team', and the story of Topiwalo provide ideal subjects for dramatisation.

The story of Topiwalo could also be used to introduce children to the traditional head-dress featured in the tale, the pupils making their own and using them to re-enact the story.

What makes a good team?

Follow-up work to the 'Tangram' and 'Jesus's team' assemblies can provoke useful discussion on the necessary components of a successful team.

Further examples of collective strength are the 'Cane demonstrations':
a) Choose about six volunteers and give each a cane. Invite two tall members of staff to hold one cane between them at shoulder height. Ask one pupil to grasp the cane in the centre and try to lift him off the floor. Invariably the cane will bend or snap under the weight. When all the canes are put together, however, the child can be lifted quite easily.
b) Demonstrate how easy it is to snap a single cane. Then put a bundle together and show how its collective strength makes it impossible to break.

What do I have to contribute?

Exercises in self-appraisal – 'I Am' – will help to raise self-esteem. The use of 'Circle time' activities, in which pupils offer their own contributions in an informal and secure setting, can be most useful in promoting positive role-models. A simple exposition can be found in *Values and Visions* by Sally Burns and Georgeanne Lamont, Hodder and Stoughton.

Many schools have 'celebration assemblies', in which a range of pupil achievements are recognised by the school community. This is a means of promoting positive attitudes and raising self-esteem. Rewarding individual progress at such an assembly might well fall within the remit of the school's behavioural policy.

Visiting speakers

The Overland Launch by C. Walter Hodges (G Bell and sons, 1969) is a great story of teamwork, and could be followed up with a visit from a representative of the RNLI, who could present a modern perspective of the work of a lifeboat station. This in turn could form part of a class, year group or school topic on the emergency services, involving visits to the local fire or police stations.

World community

Schools may wish to celebrate 'One world week' (held at the end of October). After researching different countries, collating facts, making flags or collecting artefacts, children could share their findings in a celebratory assembly.

The school team

In many schools, members of staff share personal effects (favourite music, memories, collectibles, books, poems) with the rest of the school community during assembly.

The school 'Orchestra'

Musical activity provides an ideal opportunity to demonstrate the harmonious integration of instruments and their sounds. Visiting musicians might stimulate classroom workshop sessions, in which children make their own instruments, compose music and work co-operatively to produce mini-orchestras.

Additional resources and booklists relating to **Citizenship** in primary schools can be obtained from Professor Ken Fogelman, The Centre for Citizenship Studies in Education, University of Leicester, School of Education, 21 University Road, Leicester, LE1 7RF.

Chapter 3

Come Ye Thankful People Come

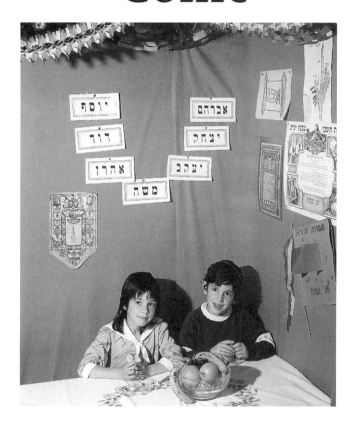

Most schools maintain the custom of celebrating Harvest Festival early in the Autumn term. Although traditional food production (ploughing, sowing and harvesting) is outside the experience of many modern children, the festival can highlight a number of issues of contemporary importance.

Historical background to Harvest Festival

The celebration of Harvest in Britain dates back to pre-Christian times when the success of the crop governed the lives of the people. Saxon farmers offered the first cut sheaf of corn to one of their gods of fertility, in order to safeguard a good harvest the following year. The last sheaf was thought to contain the Spirit of the Corn, and its cutting was usually accompanied by the ritual sacrifice of an animal – often a hare caught hiding in the corn. Later, a model hare, made from straw, was used to represent the continuity of the Spirit. This practice eventually led to the making of plaited 'corn dollies', symbolising the goddess of the grain. These were hung from the rafters in farmhouses until the next year. When the harvest was in, a celebratory supper was held to which the whole community was invited.

The now widespread practice of celebrating Harvest Festival in churches began in 1843, when the reverend Robert Hawker invited parishioners to a special thanksgiving service at his church at Morwenstow in Cornwall. This led to the long-practised custom of decorating churches with home-grown produce, beautifully described in this extract from Laurie Lee's *Cider with Rosie.*

> From our seats in the choir we watched the year turn: Christmas, Easter and Whitsun, Rogation Sunday and prayers for rain, the church following the plough very close.
>
> Harvest Festival was perhaps the one we liked best, the one that came nearest home. Then how heavily and abundantly was our small church loaded; the cream of the valley was used to decorate it. Everyone brought of his best from field and garden; and to enter the church on harvest morning was like crawling into a horn of plenty, a bursting granary, a vegetable stall, a grotto of bright flowers. The normally bare walls sprouted leaves and fruits, the altar great stooks of wheat, and ornamental loaves as big as cartwheels stood parked by the communion rails. Bunches of grapes from the squire's own vines hung blue from the lips of the pulpit. Gigantic and useless marrows abounded, leeks and onions festooned the pews, there were eggs and butter on the lectern shelves, the windows were heaped with apples, and the fat round pillars which divided the church were skirted with oats and barley.
>
> *Laurie Lee*

Sukkot

The celebration of harvest is common to many cultures and one of the most familiar is Sukkot, the **Jewish festival of the Tabernacles**.

This recalls God's care for the Israelites during their wanderings in the wilderness, after Moses had led them out of captivity in Egypt. During this period, the Hebrews had led a nomadic existence living in makeshift shelters, or sukkahs, made of branches, leaves and possibly animal skins. Once settled in Canaan, they remembered the privations of their desert journey and gave thanks to God for his protection and the bounty of their new land. These celebrations became established in the Jewish calendar, occurring five days after the October fast of Yom Kippur (the Day of Atonement), when Jews repent their shortcomings and seek to 'desert wrongdoing by returning to the Lord'.

After the meal at the end of Yom Kippur, some families put up the first post of a sukkah as a reminder that the joyful festival of Sukkot is approaching. They then share in building the fragile little shelters decorated with leaves, fruits, vegetables and flowers. The flimsy construction reminds Jews of the hard lives of their forefathers, the temporal nature of life itself, and their dependence upon God's eternal protection. Meals are taken in the sukkah, and include the freshly baked hallah or plaited loaves which are part of the traditional Sabbath Eve meal. Blessings are given to God using the 'four species', a symbolic selection of leaves and fruit comprising lulav (the shoot of a young palm tree), etrog (a citron or large lemon), hadas (myrtle leaves), and arava (willow leaves). The objects probably symbolise the end of the final harvest of the year, although another interpretation suggests that the lulav represents the spine; the myrtle, the eye; the willow, the lips; and the etrog, the heart. When they are held together in the ceremony they signify the need to serve God with one's entire being.

On the eighth day of the festival, a service in the synagogue is marked by memorial prayers for the dead and a prayer called Geshem (a prayer for rain), as in Israel, the Jews traditional homeland, spring crops depend on autumn rain. On the final day, the Torah (the holy scroll containing the law of Judaism), is taken out of the Aron Hakodesh (holy ark) and carried in a procession around the synagogue, accompanied by singing and dancing.

> *I will plant in the wilderness the cedar,*
> *The acacia tree, the myrtle, and the oil tree;*
> *I will set in the desert the cypress, the plane tree,*
>   *and the larch together;*
> *That they may see, and know and consider and*
>   *understand together,*
> *That the hand of the Lord hath done this,*
> *And the Holy One of Israel hath created this.*
> *(Isaiah 41:18–20)*

In common with many festivals celebrated by the different world faiths, the date of Sukkot can vary from year to year. A Festivals Calendar, updated annually, can be obtained from The Mobile Education Project, PO Box 326, Leicester, LE4 8PG (tel. 0116 2697209).

Harvest and the world community

Many schools use Harvest Festival to focus attention upon problems in the wider world. The following stories can be used to investigate issues of PSE, and to increase children's awareness of the inequality in the distribution of the world's resources.

The rainbow people

This story explores the conflict between self-interest and co-operation.

Characters: Narrator 1 and Narrator 2, groups of Reds, Blues, Yellows, Stranger

Narrator 1

In the beginning, the world was very still and quiet. One day a wind blew over the land. It warmed the people and filled them with life and love. They began to move ... to look at each other ... to speak to each other ... to learn about each other.

Narrator 2

As they explored their world they found coloured ribbons lying on the ground. They were excited and ran about collecting them up ... some chose blue ... some red ... some green ... some yellow ...They enjoyed tying the ribbons around each other and laughing at the bright colours.

Narrator 1

Suddenly another wind blew. This time it made them shiver with cold ...They looked at each other ... realised they looked different ... and stopped trusting each other.

The reds gathered together and ran into a corner.

Narrator 2

The blues gathered together and ran into a corner.

Narrator 1

The greens gathered together and ran into a corner.

Narrator 2

The yellows gathered together and ran into a corner.

Narrator 1

They forgot they had been friends and had cared for each other. The other colours just seemed strange and different. They built walls to separate themselves and keep the others out.

Narrator 2

But they found that ...

Narrator 1

The reds had water but no food.

Narrator 2

The blues had food but no water.

Narrator 1

The greens had twigs to make fire but no shelter.

Narrator 2

The yellows had shelter but nothing to keep them warm.

Narrator 1

Suddenly a stranger appeared and stood in the centre of the land. He looked in amazement at the people, and the walls separating them, and said loudly,

Stranger

Come on out everybody. What are you afraid of? Let's talk to each other.

Narrator 2

The people peeped out at him and slowly came out of their corners, into the centre.

Stranger

Now just tell each other what you have to give, and what you need to be given.

Blues

We have plenty of food to give but we need water.

Reds

We have plenty of water to give, but we need food.

Greens

We have plenty of wood for fire, but we need shelter.

Yellows

We have plenty of shelter, but we need warmth.

Stranger

Why don't you put together what you have and share it. And then you can all have enough to eat, drink, keep warm and have shelter.

Narrator 1

They talked and the feeling of love returned. They remembered that they had once been companions. They knocked down the walls and welcomed each other as old friends. When they realised that the colours had been divided, they wanted to throw them away. But they knew they would miss the richness of the bright colours.

Narrator 2

So instead they mixed the colours to make a beautiful rainbow.

And the rainbow became a symbol of peace and togetherness.

(This theme is developed further in *'Barriers and Bridges'*, from The Johnny Morris Storybook, BBC, and *'Two Donkeys and a Bridge'* by Ralph Steadman, Andersen Press).

The long chopsticks

There are many different versions of this story, some of which replace the chopsticks with long spoons, but the powerful moral remains the same: 'fair shares for all'.

A very long time ago, in a far off land, there lived a young prince called Lin Sung. As he travelled the country he became more and more distressed by the poverty and hunger he saw, and resolved that when he became master of the kingdom, things would change.

He told his father of his plans.

'When I'm emperor,' he vowed,' I'll do everything in my power to make sure there is enough food for everyone. No one will starve.'

The old man smiled.

'I am proud to hear these words,' he said kindly. 'I had such dreams myself when I was young. But it is so much harder to make them come true.'

His son did not understand.

'Surely if there is enough food to go around, then nobody need starve.'

The emperor nodded.

'So it would appear,' he replied sadly. 'But one day you will see.'

Some years later the old man died and the gods sent a messenger down to Earth to guide him to the gates of heaven.

'When my father passed away,' the emperor said, 'the messenger allowed me to accompany him on his last journey. I wonder if my own son might travel with me now?'

'You have led a good and honourable life, your excellency,' the messenger answered. 'I will grant your request.'

But instead of travelling straight to heaven, the emperor asked the guide to take them to the underworld, that dreadful place where troubled souls from Earth must spend eternity.

As they peered into the dark, crowded room, they beheld a wretched sight. Everyone was thin and sad, and the air was filled with the sounds of arguing and fighting.

'Look carefully, Lin Sung, and see why they quarrel.'

The young man saw long, wide tables piled high with food. There was plenty for everyone, but the people were trying to eat with chopsticks, two metres long. Once they had picked up the food they couldn't get it into their mouths to eat.

'Now let us proceed to heaven,' the old man said.

As the emperor stood outside the gates he turned to his son and smiled warmly.

'Farewell, my son,' he said. 'It is time for me to enter. Look inside and mark well what you see.'

Once more the room contained long, wide tables laden with food, exactly like those in the underworld. Once more the people were eating with chopsticks, two metres long. But this time the people were feeding each other, instead of trying to feed themselves. No one argued, or quarrelled ... nobody went hungry.

And as he returned to earth, Lin Sung finally understood his father's words.

(Rewritten from a traditional story)

Elleni and the Sharing Bread

This story addresses the issue of prejudice, and promotes mutual support.

Narrator 1, Narrator 2, Elleni, Allarik, Elleni's mother, Jan, Lana, Brendik, Villagers, Elleni's mother, Stranger

Narrator 1

The story goes that once upon a time, at the foot of a great mountain, there were two villages, one each side of a mighty river.

Narrator 2

The people of each village hated each other with a great hatred. No boats crossed the water that rushed between them. And if the other village was mentioned at all, it was with a curse.

Narrator 1

Elleni, the youngest daughter of the village chief, Allarik, could not understand why.

Elleni

How did the hatred begin, father?

Allarik

Questions, always questions, Elleni. It has always been so, and it will always be so.

Elleni's mother

Be grateful that you live in this village and not the other, Elleni.

Narrator 2

She asked her older brothers and sisters as they helped to bring in the harvest from the fields under the mountains.

Elleni

How did the hatred begin?

Jan

Oh, I heard it was a quarrel between two brothers. One took his family across to the other side and never came back. A long time ago now.

Lana

They stole grain in the night. That's how it started. Of course we have all the best wheat fields on our side.

Jan

They're a bad lot, Elleni. They do strange and wicked things. Forget about them!

Narrator 1

It was that year that great fear came down from the

mountain. It was brought by Brendik, the youngest of the shepherds. He ran through the fields shouting to the villagers who were now bringing in the last of the wheat.

Brendik

Danger, danger! Quick, run back to the village as fast as you can. Danger, danger!

Narrator 2

He staggered into the village and into the Hall of Meetings where he rang the summoning bell.

Brendik

There is danger. We must move out of the village.

Allarik

What do you mean? What's happened?

Brendik

In the night there was a terrible noise, like thunder. Stones, boulders, came rushing down the mountainside and blocked the stream that runs into our river. A deep lake is building up, crushing against the rocks. Soon it will all come bursting through. We must move out. The water is pushing against the stones. It could break through on the east side, and come crashing down on us, or ...

Villagers

Go on, go on!

Brendik

Or if it breaks through the western ridge it will fall on the other village.

Allarik

Come everyone. There is no time to lose. Pack your belongings, everything you value. We must climb the South hill to safety. We'll camp there until the mountains decide between us.

Elleni

But father, shouldn't we warn the other villagers too?

Allarik

Are you mad, girl? Let them look after themselves. Help your mother and sisters pack the food. Warn the other villagers? Whatever next?

Narrator 1

The villagers collected their goods and climbed to the top of the South hill, where they spent the night around a camp-fire, praying and listening. On which side would the torrent of rock and flood burst through? Which village would be destroyed?

Finally the mountain made up its mind.

The waters crashed through and poured down on the other village.

Narrator 2

Laughing and singing, the villagers on South hill gathered their belongings and congregated at the Hall of Meetings before returning to the safety of their homes. The village chief addressed them.

Allarik

Finish bringing in the wheat. Return here this afternoon. We'll have the Sharing Bread and then our harvest feast.

Narrator 2

At home, Elleni's mother prepared the traditional meal, but this year there was additional reason for celebration.

Elleni's mother

Elleni, hurry and grind that corn. The flour is needed for the Sharing Bread. Stop daydreaming, girl.

Elleni

I'm thinking about those people in the other village. I can't get them out of my mind. What has happened to them?

Elleni's mother

Think what will happen to you if that flour is not ready. It's your turn to present the bread in the Hall of Meetings this afternoon. Will you bring disgrace upon your father's house?

Narrator 1

The Hall of Meetings was full. Everyone was ready to present their harvest gifts.

(At this point of a Harvest service children could bring their own produce to the front.)

Narrator 2

All the gifts were received. Allarik, the chief, stood before the villagers.

Allarik

Let us give praise and thanks for our harvest and our safety. Elleni, bring the Sharing Bread. Each family will break off a piece and each member will share it. But take one piece back with you to place beneath your hearth-stone to give you good fortune throughout the coming year.

(Noises off. Everyone looks to the door as a ragged, exhausted stranger enters.)

Stranger

Please help us. We have nothing. Our houses have all gone. Many are dead, others lie trapped in the ruins;

children scream for their missing parents. Even the living will soon die if we don't get food ... and you have ... all this! I swam across the swollen river. You must help us!

(Elleni steps forward.)

Elleni

Here, share our bread.

Allarik

Oh my people, we are in great shame for the terrible thing we have done. It has taken a child to show us what lay buried in our hearts. We have done you, friend, a great wrong. Forgive us.

There will be no celebrating here until the other village is fed. Let none share this food who does not also share this promise. Let us take our boats and cross the river. We will give all the help we can before returning with our neighbours for the feast.

(Villagers leave; Elleni holds Sharing Bread, and kneels in prayer.)

(Adapted from *Elleni and the Sharing Bread* by Arthur Scholey).

ADDITIONAL RESOURCES:

Mother Earth, Nancy Luenn, Letterbox Library
The Farmer's Gift', Andre Deutsch

Songs and rhymes for Harvest

The dingle dangle scarecrow

Chorus
I'm a dingle dangle scarecrow
with a flippy, floppy hat,
I can shake my hands like this,
I can shake my hands like that.

Verse 1
When all the cows were sleeping
And the sun had gone to bed
Up jumped the scarecrow
And this is what he said ...

Chorus

Verse 2
When all the hens were roosting
And the moon behind a cloud,
Up jumped the scarecrow
And shouted very loud ...

Chorus

Oats, peas, beans, and barley grow

Oats, peas, beans, and barley grow,
Oats, peas, beans and barley grow,
Do you or I or any one know
How oats, peas, beans, and barley grow?

Thus the farmer sows his seed,
Stands erect and takes his ease,
He stamps his foot and claps his hands,
And turns around to view his lands.

Waiting for a partner,
Waiting for a partner,
Open the ring and take her in,
While we all gaily dance and sing.

Now you're married you must obey,
You must be true to all you say,
You must be kind, you must be good,
And make your husband chop the wood!

Arranged by Norman Lloyd

Activities

Dramatisation of stories

Several of the stories in this chapter have been adapted into playlets.

Follow-up activities

PSE issues originating from the stories can be developed in class discussions, and could be linked to several of the activities listed below.

Art and craft / design technology

There are numerous opportunities for artwork deriving from the material in this chapter. Wall displays can reflect the varied nature of harvest activities – the harvest of the land; the harvest of the sea; the harvest of the earth; 3-D pictures composed using autumn fruits and seeds, and collections of corn dollies.

Miniature sukkahs can be constructed using shoe boxes or cardboard cartons, or a larger school version built and decorated by representatives of each class. This could provide an impressive focal point if supported by artefacts relating to the Jewish faith.

One school effectively used the aerial view of a patchworked landscape to develop a theme based on the song 'From a distance', creating collage pictures in string to represent the different crops growing in the fields. (The definitive version of 'From a Distance' can be found on a CD entitled 'The Best of Nanci Griffiths'.)

(Celebration and Multi-Faith boxes are available from Budget Paper Supplies Ltd, Arborfield Mill, Helpston, Peterborough, PE6 7DH, tel. 01733 252868.)

Children can also design and distribute invitations to parents and guests for the Harvest service.

Harvest food

One of the most rewarding activities is to bake **harvest loaves**. Children can also contribute to a harvest 'basket of life' in which individual qualities and virtues can be displayed alongside the fruit, flowers and vegetables.

Charitable agencies

The disposal of produce donated to the Harvest Festival service can involve supporting charitable agencies involved in famine relief, or similar work, in deprived areas of the world.
It is often helpful to invite a representative of the agency into assembly, to explain to the pupils how their contribution will be used.

Useful contact addresses:

Oxfam, 274 Banbury Road, Oxford OX2 7DZ
Christian Aid, P O Box 100, London SE1 7RT

Save the Children Fund, 17 Grove Lane, London, SE5 8RD
UNICEF UK, 55 Lincoln's Inn Fields London WC2A 3NB

As the Harvest Festival service occurs early in a new school term, it can provide a useful whole school focus for continuing charity work throughout the year. Many schools have adopted a particular 'good cause', placing responsibility upon pupils for the organisation of fund-raising activities. Sometimes the experiences of pupils, or people with whom the school has an association, can lead to a special relationship between the school and a specific cause.

Chapter 4

Light in Our Darkness

The symbol of light (goodness) overcoming darkness (evil) is common to many faiths and cultures, and central to numerous celebrations held during the autumn.

Both Hindus and Sikhs celebrate **Divali** (festival of lights) although the origins of the celebrations differ considerably.

The **Hindu** Divali, which marks the beginning of the religious new year, commemorates the victory of Rama over the demon king, Ravana, and his triumphant return from exile. The story of Rama's life and heroism is the subject of the Ramayana, a great epic poem comprising 24,000 verses and dating from the third century CE.

Rama and Sita

King Desharatha, the wise ruler of Koshola, built his palace in the northern Indian city of Ayodhya. He had three wives, and four sons named Rama, Bharata, Lakshmana and Shatrughna. Rama, the eldest, was his favourite, and had been specially chosen by the gods to fight evil in the form of Ravana, the ten-armed, ten-headed demon king and his followers. Rama grew into a brave warrior, skilled in the arts of hunting, fighting and riding, and his prowess with a bow won him the hand of Sita, daughter of King Janaka of Videha. (In those days it was customary for a princess to choose a husband from her many suitors at an archery contest.) Rama alone succeeded in bending the royal bow which had once belonged to the great god Shiva. He married Sita and for a time they were very happy, indeed the three other brothers agreed that Rama and Sita would be the perfect rulers of the kingdom when their father died. Rama's stepmother, Kaikeyi, however, had other ideas. She wanted her son, Bharata, to inherit the throne and asked Desharatha to grant her two wishes promised many years before. She demanded that Bharata be made king and Rama banished to the forest for fourteen years. The king knew he could not go back on a promise and reluctantly carried out Kaikeyi's request. Rama obeyed his father's command and took Sita, and Lakshmana, his best-loved brother, with him into exile.

When Desharatha died soon afterwards, of a broken heart, Bharata went into the forest to ask the rightful king to return. Rama refused, complying with his father's orders. Bharata went back to Ayodhya, bearing his brother's golden sandals, which he placed on the throne as a sign that he would govern the country wisely until Rama returned.

Rama, Sita and Lakshmana had lived happily in the forest for ten years when the evil Ravana made his fateful appearance. The demon king had devised a plan to kidnap the princess and carry her off to his palace on the island of Sri Lanka. Ravana changed one of his demons into a beautiful golden deer, knowing that Rama, a keen hunter, would seek to capture the creature for his wife. Cunningly, the deer lured the prince deeper into the forest, ever further from the shelter where Sita was waiting. Ravana then tricked Lakshmana into following his brother, breached the magic circle drawn around the hut to protect Sita, and kidnapped her. On their return, Rama and Lakshmana were distressed to find the shelter empty and set out to search for the missing princess. After numerous thrilling adventures in which many wrongs were righted and brave deeds done, they gained the help of Hanuman, the famous monkey-warrior. Together they built a bridge of rocks from the mainland to Ravana's castle and launched their rescue mission. Rama killed Ravana with an arrow fired from a special bow, the demon king's forces were routed, Sita was saved, and the victors returned to the kingdom of Ayodhya in triumph.

Bharata, who had carried out his promise to preserve the throne until his brother's return, ordered that all buildings be decorated with flags and garlands, and that thousands of small lamps, or divas, should be lit throughout the city to guide the rightful king and his queen back home to their palace.

Rama and Sita were crowned shortly afterwards, and ruled their kingdom wisely and well for many years.

Hindus believe Sita to be the earthly manifestation of Lakshmi, the consort of Vishnu the sun-god. Worship at the mandir on the eve of Divali is especially devoted to Lakshmi, who is believed to bring 'health, power, victory and happiness to all those upon whom she smiles'.

On Divali itself, the temple is brightly decorated and filled with lighted candles, symbolising the triumph of light over darkness, good over evil, and providing a reminder of the better side of human nature.

Sikhs celebrate Divali by commemorating the arrival in Amritsar, the city of the sacred Golden Temple, of Guru Har Gobind, the sixth Guru, in the early seventeenth century CE.

Guru Har Gobind had been released from captivity by the Mughal emperor Jehangir after charges against him of treason were proven unfounded. He refused to accept his freedom, however, unless 52 innocent Hindu princes were also set free. The emperor decreed that only as many princes as could pass through the narrow passage of the jail while holding the Guru's cloak would be released. Guru Har Gobind asked for a cloak with 52 tassels, and by each holding on to one of these, all the princes gained their freedom.

To celebrate the story, Sikhs light up the whole of the Golden Temple complex and enjoy spectacular firework displays illuminating the night sky. Treasure and weapons used by the Gurus are exhibited, while in other parts of the world, candles are lit symbolising the special occasion.

Hanukkah, the **Jewish** festival of lights, celebrates the victory of Judas Maccabaeus (Judas the Hammer), and his followers over Antiochus, the Syrian ruler of Judaea, in 165 BCE.

Antiochus, having failed to coerce the Jews into giving up their faith, desecrated the Holy Temple in Jerusalem by dedicating it to the Greek god Zeus. He then ordered all Jews to worship the pagan image. When his soldiers attempted to enforce the decree, Mattathias and his five sons formed a guerrilla army of freedom fighters intent on overthrowing the Syrians. The struggle lasted over three years, but eventually the invaders were defeated and Jerusalem restored to the Jews.

An eight day long re-dedication of the Temple began, but when the

Flame of Thanksgiving was about to be relit, just one flask of holy oil was unearthed – sufficient only to keep the lamp burning for one day. Miraculously, the flame continued to burn for eight days and nights, by which time enough oil had been produced to replenish the supply.

So began the festival of Hanukkah (meaning 'dedication'), when Jews remember the re-dedication of the Temple and the triumph of good over evil.

Central to the festival is the Hanukkah menorah, a nine-branched candlestick. The festival lasts eight days so there is one candle for each day, and the other, known as the 'shammash', or 'servant candle', is used to light each of the others. A box of Hanukkah candles contains 44. One for the first day, two for the second, and so on plus one shammash for each day.

 Light is an important symbol in **Christianity**. Jesus said,

> *I am the light of the world. Whoever follows me will not walk in darkness, but will have the light of life.*

In the Sermon on the Mount, Jesus told His disciples,

> *You are the light of the world. A city that is set on a hill cannot be hidden.*
>
> *Men do not light a candle and put it under a bushel, but on a candlestick, where it gives light to all that are in the house.*
>
> *Let your light shine before men that they may see your good works, and glorify your Father who is in heaven.'*

(Matthew 5: 14–16)

During Advent, the four-week period leading up to Christmas, Christians light five candles – one on each of the four Sundays before Christmas, and the last on Christmas Day itself. The end of the festive period is marked by **Candlemas Eve**, which is celebrated on 1 February.

In ancient times, candles were thought of as off-shoots of the life-giving sun and were believed to give protection against famine, plague and other disasters. In pagan celebrations, such as the Feast of Lights in honour of the Earth goddess, Ceres, and the Roman festival of Februa, candles were often carried in a procession. Perhaps that is why the early Christian church introduced candles into its own ceremony at this time of year.

At Candlemas, churches are decorated with candles which are blessed and distributed amongst the congregation. The festival recalls the presentation of the infant Jesus by His parents at the Temple in Jerusalem, and their meeting with two old holy people, Anna and Simeon. When Simeon saw the baby he said,

> *Mine eyes have seen thy salvation, which thou hast*

prepared before the face of all people; to be a light to lighten the Gentiles, and the glory of thy people Israel.

ADDITIONAL RESOURCES:

Festivals, Jean Gilbert, OUP, includes a detailed section on Divali and Hanukkah, containing a wealth of music, dance and poetry.
India: Activities and Projects in Colour, Claude Sobillant, Blandford Press
Indian Music (Oxford Topics in Music), Leile Floyd, OUP
Catalogue of Indian publications available from Soma Books, 38 Kennington Lane, London SE11 4LS (tel. 0171 735 2101)
Lights for Gita, Rachna Gilmore, Second Story Press
Divali slide set and other materials available from Minority Group Support Services, Prior Deram Walk, Canley, Coventry CV4 8FT (tel. 01203 717800)
A book of Chanukah, KTAV Publications, available from Jewish Memorial Council Bookshop, Woburn House, Upper Woburn Place, London WC1 (tel. 0171 724 7778)
Christian Education Movement, Royal Buildings, Victoria Street, Derby DE1 1GW. (tel. 01332 296655)

The story of light

One of the many folk-tales from around the world to explore the origin of light is this evocative version of a Cherokee Indian myth.

It was dark ...

before the sun came. The animal people couldn't see, though they had heard the sun was alive on the other side of the world. They met together in darkness, bumping into each other, stepping on each other's animal feet; and they decided it was foolish to keep living in such darkness when all they had to do was take some of the sun for themselves.

But which one of them would go? Bear lumbered into the animals' circle. He was eager to help his friends and he never thought too long about anything. 'I'll get the sun,' said Bear. 'Wait just a minute,' said Fox. 'You might need an ounce of my cunning. I'll go.' But when he jumped up to leave, two yellow eyes blocked his way on the pitch-black path. 'This job is mine,' said Wolf. All the animals cried, 'Never you, Wolf!' Wolf was a wanderer. Once Wolf got the sun, who knew if he'd ever return?

Then Possum loomed thick in the middle of the crowd. 'I'll snatch a speck of the sun,' he said. 'I'll hide it in my great bushy tail.' The animals agreed that Possum should go. So Possum walked east to the other side of the world, squinting with pain, squeezing his eyes shut as the brightness burned and burned even when his eyes were tightly closed.

He shielded his scorched eyes with his sweating paw. And still feeling fire and fear, he came to the sun's spot. His parched mouth said: O.

Possum stole a spark of white-hot sun and stuck it under his beautiful tail. It singed his fur as he scurried home to the animal people. But when he returned, the spark had gone out and all that remained was his charred black snake of a tail, and ...

it was still dark.

Buzzard thought he knew better. 'I'll keep that sun far away from my sleek tail feathers,' he said. He smiled a little, secretly musing on how much cleverer than Possum he would be. 'I'll bring sunlight home high on the top of my feathery head.' And he left, flying east to the other side of the world.

He soon snatched a bit of the sun in his big strong claws and he placed it on top of his feathery head.

But the spark set a feather on fire, then another then another, and by the time he got home there were no feathers left on the top of his head, only ash; the spark had burnt out, and ...

it was still dark.

'Let me try,' called the smallest of voices.

'Let me try,' the voice insisted. It was only Spider, swinging above all the animal people.

'You? You're too small,' said the bears. 'And too old,' said the foxes. 'You're a woman,' said the wolves.

'Never mind that,' called out Spider. She swung down to the earth, took damp clay, and with her tiny hands she moulded a pot. Then she walked to the east, spinning her thread, and she followed the rays of the sun as they bent to lead her through the shadowy grass.

Spider's pot first turned leather-hard in the cool dark of her slow walk. And as the day grew lighter and hotter, so the pot grew harder and drier.

It was a long walk for Spider. At the sun's spot she took the smallest of sparks to hide in her little clay pot. She turned around slowly and followed her thread back to the west, lighting her way with the sun in her pot.

And this was how Spider brought the sun to her animal people. It's The Story of Light ...

And even today Possum shuns the sun; he still has a tail with no fur; and Buzzard still has a head with no feathers; and Spider's webs still look like sun's rays; and pots are still dried slowly in the shadows before they are baked in a very hot oven.

Susan Roth

With a single copper coin

This traditional story contains a spiritual dimension.

King Hitesh was proud of his two sons, Rakan and Pratibah. They had grown into strong, handsome and brave warriors. Both were daring riders, fine archers and skilled swordsmen. But Hitesh knew that the gift of wisdom was more important to a good king than skills in the art of war, so he decided to set his sons a test to determine which would rule the kingdom most wisely upon his death.

Late one evening, he summoned the two young men and explained their task.

'Tomorrow morning,' he said, 'before the sun rises, you will go to market and purchase something that will completely fill this great hall. Whoever buys most wisely will succeed me as king when I am dead.'

And with this, he handed each a single copper coin of very small value.

He wished them both goodnight and went to bed, leaving the princes to ponder what they could possibly buy, with a single copper coin, to fill the vast room in which they stood.

Early next morning the brothers explored the market, each desperately seeking that wise purchase. There was no shortage of goods. Stalls and wagons were loaded with produce, but everything seemed to cost much more than a single copper coin. As Pratibah wandered up and down the rows of tables, piled high with fruit and vegetables, he began to despair. His single coin would buy enough to cover a solitary floor tile in the great hall, no more. The day passed and the prince prepared to return to the palace empty handed, when he saw a cart stacked high with straw. The farmer had also suffered a poor day at market and was only too pleased to sell as much straw as the prince could carry for a single copper coin. The young man hoisted several bales on his powerful shoulders, and set off for the great hall, where he spread the straw as thickly as possible over the floor. But, hard as he tried, it barely reached the bottom of the windows set halfway up the walls. All he could hope was that his brother had fared less well.

It was after sunset when Rakan arrived. He carried nothing in his hands save the leather pouch which had held the copper coin. When he opened the bag, however, he revealed the one thing which would completely fill the great hall. His father was truly pleased.

'Pratibah has demonstrated great perseverance and initiative, both useful qualities in a king. But you, Rakan, have shown wisdom and that is the greatest gift of all. You are the worthy successor to my kingdom.'

> Rakan then took the candle, which he had bought with his single copper coin, and placed it carefully in the middle of the huge room. As the flame flickered brightly, its glow reached even the darkest corners, and filled the king's great hall with light.
>
> *(Adapted from a traditional Indian folk-tale)*

Activities

Hallowe'en

Hallowe'en, and its association with witchcraft and the occult, has its origins in the ancient Celtic feast of Samain. This was celebrated on 31 October and 1 November, marking the end of the year's cycle of agricultural work, when fires were lit to boost the dying sun and ward off spirits and demons released by Samain, the Lord of Death.

The festival was 'Christianised' and converted into the three-day Hallow-tide ('hallow' meaning to make holy) in memory of the Christian dead – All Hallows Eve, All Hallows or All Saints Day and All Souls Day.

Much to the disapproval of the Church these pagan practices, intended to protect families from evil forces, continued: bonfires were lit and windows decorated with lanterns and candles.

Hallowe'en, with its 'trick or treat' over-commercialisation, and an alleged increase in satanic activity, has recently caused many schools to limit or even abandon any celebration of the ancient festival.

Bonfire night

On 5 November it is still customary to commemorate, with bonfires and firework displays, the failed attempt to assassinate King James I in 1605. Effigies of Guy Fawkes, one of the chief plotters, are often burned on the fires. However, the authenticity of the traditional version of the Gunpowder Plot story has recently been brought into question. Modern-day parallels with terrorism linked to religious intolerance require that schools deal sensitively with the subject, and teachers may prefer to under-emphasise the political aspects in favour of the wealth of opportunities the occasion affords for cross-curricular work, with poetry as a possible stimulus.

Fireworks

They rise like sudden fiery flowers
That burst upon the night,
Then fall to earth in burning showers
Of crimson, blue and white.

Like buds too wonderful to name,
Each miracle unfolds,
And catherine-wheels begin to flame
Like whirling marigolds.

Rockets and Roman candles make
An orchard in the sky,
Whence magic trees their petals shake
Upon each gazing eye.

James Reeves

The above poem comes from the *Poetry Plus* series, (Schofield and Sims), which contains a wide selection of poems about Bonfire night.

Stained glass windows

The sun's rays streaming through stained glass effectively demonstrates of the symbolic use of light in religious architecture and design. Church buildings, from world famous cathedrals to the humblest parish churches and chapels, contain hugely impressive windows, often rich in history.

Divali

Many schools now enjoy the Divali celebrations as the colourful festival provides opportunities for a variety of activities. Links can be developed with representatives of the local mandir, who will often visit schools to organise a structured programme comprising music, dance, a study of traditional designs and patterns, and cooking from Indian recipes.

The story of Rama and Sita can be dramatised, set to music, or used as a stimulus for painting and craft activity.

Children can compile an exhibition of lamps and lights, representing the 'divas' that are central to the Divali story.

Divas can be made by kneading together flour, water and a little dough, to which yellow food colouring is added. This is moulded into a circular shape with a hole in the middle. In this is placed a wick of cotton wool soaked in ghee (melted butter). The lamps can then be arranged in dishes, displayed around the room, and lit.

Festival Food

Children will enjoy making Parshad, the traditional Sikh sweet passed around among worshippers at the end of services in the gurdwara.

Parshad

Ingredients:

one cup sugar
one cup melted butter
one cup wholemeal flour

Method:

Put the sugar and some water into a saucepan and simmer until the sugar has been dissolved.
Mix the butter and flour in another saucepan and fry until the flour is golden brown.

Add the sweet, warm water to the flour and cook on a low heat, stirring continuously until the mixture becomes very thick.
Leave to cool and set for at least half an hour before serving.

Potato latkes

Latkes (potato pancakes) are a traditional food at Hanukkah.

Ingredients:

0.5 kg potatoes
one medium onion
one teaspoon salt
one teaspoon pepper
one egg (beaten)
one tablespoon flour
oil, for frying

Method:

Grate the potatoes, squeeze out the juice, grate the onion and mix the ingredients together. Heat the oil in a frying pan and put large spoonfuls of the mixture into it. Fry until it is brown on both sides, then remove it and drain.
It is customary to eat the latkes with apple sauce or sour cream.

(from Hanukkah, Leila Berg, Ginn)

The dreidel

During the Jewish festival of Hanukkah, many families continue the custom of playing games of chance using a kind of spinning top called a dreidel. This is a four-sided spinning top with a Hebrew letter on each side – the Hebrew equivalent of 'n', 'g', 'h', and 'sh'. These stand for the Hebrew phrase Nes gadol haya sham: 'A great miracle happened there'. In this game the letters stand for *nichts* (nothing), *ganz* (all), *halb* (half) and *shtell ein* (put one in).

Players each begin the game with an identical pile of nuts or sweets and spin the dreidel to see how many to put in the middle or take from the middle.

Dance

This simple dance was devised by a student on school experience with Year 1 pupils to support a class project on 'Light'. The children interpret sources of light through a variety of movements.

OBJECTIVES:

* to listen to given instructions and respond accordingly;
* to explore diverse movements using different parts of the body to imitate different sources of light;
* to link movements to form simple dance.

ACTIVITY/STRATEGY:

* Warm-up activities
* Discuss sources of light / identify natural phenomena, ie sun, moon, stars. The children will then interpret each one by using different movements.

    Sun – The children start curled up small on the floor, then gradually unfold, bending upwards. Standing straight, they move their arms in a large circular motion, wiggling fingers to show the sun's rays shining.
    Moon – The children stand up straight, then bend the top half of their bodies over, placing their hands together so their bodies form crescent moon shapes.
    Stars – Children use the whole body to show the stars twinkling, including wiggling fingers.

* Discuss artificial / man-made sources of light and interpret in movement.

    Torch – With arms out in front, children walk in straight lines demonstrating the path taken by light.
    Candle – Arms should point above head; swing them to and fro, suggesting the flickering flame.
    Electricity – Children could shake their bodies quickly, when the leader shouts 'on'; sink to floor when the leader shouts 'off'.
    Street lamps – Children stand up straight, bending arms over.

* Discuss the movement of the Earth and other planets around the sun;
* Listen to appropriate music (e.g. 'Venus' *The Planets* suite by Gustav Holst);
* Link movements practised for all the light sources and perform as below.

    Sun→Moon→Stars – move around the room. Candle – melt into a small shape, and lie flat on the floor. Shoulder tap, children follow around room, twinkling, leading into circle (repeat).

Cross curricular activities

Stained glass windows made from tissue or oil-based paper can create impressive displays, linking easily into cross-curricular projects related to local history and the community.

The Lighthouse Keeper's Lunch, by Ronda and David Armitage (Andre Deutsch 1997) can provide a useful introduction to technology activities involving the construction of model lighthouses, and incorporating simple electrical circuits, pulleys and winches. This enjoyable cross-curricular topic can be adapted to involve all the children across Key Stage 1.

Language
1 Drama
Build up events leading to the final downfall of the seagulls
2 Speaking and Listening/Writing
Viewpoint of Hamish the cat
Poems about food
How would you scare away the seagulls?
Viewpoint of the seagulls

Technology
1 Create a lighthouse with a rope and a pulley leading to the white cottage on the cliffs.
2 Design a bag or basket to carry Mr Grinling's packed lunch.
3 Create own packed lunch, i.e. making bread and butter, choosing favourite fillings for sandwiches, making cakes

Follow-up books
The Lighthouse Keeper's Catastrophe
The Lighthouse Keeper's Rescue

Useful items for use in technology work can be obtained from:
Teaching Technology Systems, Unit 4, Park Road, Holmeworth, Chesterfield   S42 5UY (tel. 01246 850085). Teachers might also refer to the booklet, *Be Safe! Some aspects of safety in school science and technology for key stages 1 and 2*, published by The Association for Science Education 1990.

Chapter 5

Remembrances

The theme of remembrance can embrace a wide range of topics, many of which provide excellent opportunities for cross-curricular work.

Remembrance Day

At 11 am on the eleventh day of November 1918, the guns were finally silenced as an armistice brought the First World War to an end. Described as 'the war to end all wars', the conflict was one of the most terrible in history, with both sides suffering huge losses on the Western Front (a vast network of trenches which extended across northern France and Belgium, creating a stalemate in which the opposing armies conducted a campaign of attrition). Hard-won territory was frequently lost within days, and battles raged over the same ground throughout the four years of war. The outdated 'one last push' strategy, frequently employed by Chiefs of Staff on both sides, contributed to the mass slaughter.

The Battle of the Somme provides a graphic example of this. On the morning of 1 July 1916, after a week-long bombardment of enemy lines, thousands of troops climbed from their dugouts and walked across 'no-man's land', between the trenches, into a hail of shelling and machine gun fire. The Allies suffered 60,000 casualties on that terrible first day of the battle.

When peace finally arrived, the British Legion was formed to help soldiers badly disabled in the fighting. As the anniversary of the armistice approached, replica poppies were sold to raise money for the cause – a reminder of the flowers which grew in profusion on the battlefields.

> *In Flanders fields the poppies grow*
> *Among the crosses, row on row.*

Sadly, the hopes that such dreadful happenings would bring conflict to an end were not realised, and on 3 September 1939, Europe was plunged into darkness once more.

The Second World War ended in 1945, but peace continues to prove both fragile and elusive.

Each year, on the second Sunday in November, special services are held in memory of those killed in conflict. The lists of dead recorded in churches and on war memorials throughout the world bear testimony to the dreadful waste of young lives.

> *They shall grow not old, as we that are left grow old:*
> *Age shall not weary them, nor the years condemn.*
> *At the going down of the sun, and in the morning*
> *We will remember them.*
>
> Laurence Binyon (1869–1943)

The poppy remains the symbol of remembrance, and money raised from the sales of replica poppies continues to provide support for both disabled survivors and the dependants of those killed in conflict.

There are many wartime stories which demonstrate the strength of the human spirit in adversity. One of the most poignant is that of Anne Frank, a young Jewish girl who recorded her experiences in a famous diary, published several years after her death in a Nazi concentration camp.

A special friend

Have you got a special friend? Someone to whom you can tell all your innermost secrets? You're lucky if you have. Such people are rare. That is why Anne was pleased with her birthday present. So pleased that she wrote, 'I hope I shall be able to confide in you completely, as I have never been able to do in anyone before, and I hope that you will be a great support and comfort to me.'

So what do you think the present was?

It was a book. A book with stiff covers and lots of empty pages. Plenty of room to write her thoughts.

Her first entry ends:

'Bye-bye, we're going to be great pals.'

And she named her special friend, Kitty.

So begins an incredible story of courage, love and eventual betrayal. The early pages are full of typical light hearted comments about family, school and friends. Anne was very much an ordinary schoolgirl, labelled a chatterer by her maths teacher. But the times were far from normal. This was Amsterdam in June 1942. Anne's parents had emigrated from Germany in 1933, the year that Adolf Hitler became Chancellor. Now Holland, like most of Western Europe, was under German occupation. Anne and her sister Margot were treated like criminals. They were required to wear a huge, yellow, six-pointed star on their clothing. They were forbidden to do those ordinary things we take for granted: travel by train, visit a cinema, swimming baths or tennis court, ride a bicycle or sit in the garden after eight o'clock in the evening. Their crime? They were Jewish. Much worse was to come. Less than a month after Anne's thirteenth birthday, Mr Frank received a call-up notice from the Gestapo, the German secret police. Anne understood what this meant. Her father must join the thousands of Jews and 'inferiors' deported to concentration camps. There he would be forced to work in a slave labour gang until starvation or execution claimed his life. Such treatment was not confined to men. No-one was spared; the whole family was at risk. So they decided to go into hiding.

Into hiding, Anne wrote. *Where would we go, to a town or the country, in a house or a cottage, when, how, where ...?*

There was only time to pack a few precious belongings – hair curlers, school books and her beloved diary.

The chosen place was the two upper back floors above the office building where her father had worked. Mr Frank had spent months preparing the hideaway and now it was ready. Anne called it the 'Secret Annexe', its entry hidden behind filing cabinets and a revolving cupboard. Here the family were to eat, sleep, and fill every minute of every day until the war was won and they could emerge in safety. Or until they were found.

Saturday, 11th July 1942. Dear Kitty,

I can't tell you how oppressive it is never to be able to go outdoors, also I'm scared to death we shall be discovered and shot ...'

The fear was very real. Even the slightest noise, a cough, a dripping tap, a dropped book could betray their position to the people working in the building downstairs.

When a plumber came to move water pipes in the office below, the family were unable to use the toilet or speak or move for the entire day.

Tension increased with the arrival of other Jewish families to share their hiding place. You can imagine what it was like if you've ever been cooped up with your brother or sister on a wet day in the holidays with nowhere to go and nothing much to do.

Saturday, 27th September 1942. Dear Kitty,

Just had a big bust-up with Mummy for the umpteenth time ... and Margot and I don't hit it off any too well either.

There were few contacts with the outside world. Food and supplies had to be carried in by Dutch friends who risked their own lives. One special helper was Miep Van Santen who worked in the office downstairs. She also brought frightening news of the fate of other Jewish families, torn apart, deprived of possessions and carted off to face certain death in the labour camps. Little wonder that Anne occasionally gave vent to feelings of despair.

Wednesday, 3rd May 1944

What, oh what is the use of war? Why can't people live peaceably together? Why all this destruction? ... Oh why are people so crazy?

Yet throughout the long hours of silence and inactivity Anne never gave up hope. She wrote about her dreams for the future, expressing her joy and gratitude for her safety and good health and the beauty of the world.

Their tiny radio set brought news of D-Day and the successful Allied invasion. Hopes were raised. Holland would soon be free again. Anne looked forward to leaving her prison of safety and hunger and returning to school. But it was not to be.

On August 4th, 1944, armed secret police raided the office and discovered the hiding place. The family had been betrayed. Everyone was arrested, packed in cattle trucks and transported to extermination centres in German-occupied Poland. Mrs Frank perished in Auschwitz. Anne and her sister Margot died in the infamous concentration camp at Belsen in February 1945.

The Secret Annexe had been plundered during the raid. Everything was removed except a pile of newspapers and a couple of notebooks, which were given by an office cleaner to Miep Van Santen who kept them hidden until the war had ended. They contained Anne's diaries.

Mr Frank, incredibly, survived the death camp, and in 1947 published his daughter's story for the world to read. One of Anne's final entries reads:

Dear Kitty,

... I want to go on living even after my death.

Her special friend ensures that she does.

Ian Addis

The Anne Frank Educational Trust has produced an information pack for schools containing differentiated material for use across the Key Stages. These are available from PO Box 432, Bushey, Herts, WD2 1QU (tel. 0181 950 6476). *The Diary of Anne Frank* was republished by Longman Imprint Books to commemorate the first national Anne Frank Day on 12 June 1996.

Fortunately, many people recall less harrowing experiences and, as the following stories indicate, it is often the unusual or bizarre wartime memory that survives.

Aftermath

I am now a great grandma of 83 years of age and have only vague memories of most of my experiences.

However, one vivid experience remains in my mind. It was when Nottingham had a nine-hour blitz, or air-raid, by enemy bombers early in May 1941.

I was 29 at the time and my husband was in the forces. My mother was in hospital and my father on duty as an air-raid warden. On hearing the sirens that warned us of the oncoming raid, I put the shutters up on all the downstairs windows because of the shrapnel that fell from the Spitfires and anti-aircraft guns defending the city.

The house was situated on a hill overlooking the forest so I went upstairs to look through the windows. I saw churches, factories and other buildings enveloped in flames!

I came downstairs to shelter beneath the dining-room table. The raid went on all through the night.

When the sirens sounded the all-clear the following morning I discovered we had no gas, no electricity and no water so I set off down the road parallel with a main road leading into the city. I was dismayed and shocked to see the devastation en route. Eventually I came to the clothes shop where I worked as an assistant only to find the doors hanging off and all the models covered in black soot! I continued working there until a few weeks later when I was directed to work for the G.P.O. for the duration of the war.

Moving away from the shop I learned the gasometers were burning at the other end of the city and, as well as numerous other buildings, Boots' new office had been bombed. All the paperwork was blown a mile across the county!

(Told to April Thompson by her great grandma)

Carrie's war

During the early days of the Second World War, thousands of children were relocated from cities into the country to escape an expected enemy bombardment. In this extract from Carrie's War, *Nina Bawden describes the misery endured by countless evacuee children as they arrived at strange destinations and waited to be 'claimed' by surrogate parents.*

'Stand by there, then,' the woman said, 'There by the wall with the others, and someone will choose you.'

Carrie looked round, bewildered, and saw Albert Sandwich. She whispered, 'What's happening?' and he said, 'A kind of cattle auction, it seems.'

He sounded calmly disgusted. He gave Carrie her suitcase, then marched to the end of the hall, sat down on his own, and took a book out of his pocket.

Carrie wished she could do that. Sit down and read as if nothing else mattered. But she had already begun to feel ill with shame at the fear that no one would choose her, the way she always felt when they picked teams at school. Suppose she was left to the last! She dragged Nick into the line of waiting children and stood, eyes on the ground, hardly daring to breathe. When someone called out, 'A nice little girl for Mrs Davies, now,' she felt she would suffocate. She looked up but unfocused her eyes so that passing faces blurred and swam in front of her.

Nick's hand tightened in hers. She looked at his white face and the traces of sick round his mouth and wanted to shake him. No one would take home a boy who looked like that, so pale and delicate. They would think he was bound to get ill and be a trouble to them. She said in a low, fierce voice, 'Why don't you smile and look nice,' and he blinked with surprise, looking so small and so sweet that she softened. She said, 'Oh it's all right, I'm not cross. I won't leave you.'

Minutes passed, feeling like hours. Children left the line and were taken away. Only unwanted ones left, Carrie thought. She and Nick, and a few tough-looking boys, and an ugly girl with a squint who had two little sisters. And Albert Sandwich who was still sitting quietly on his suitcase, reading his book and taking no notice. He didn't care! Carrie tossed her head and hummed under her breath to show she didn't either.

Someone had stopped in front of her. Someone said, 'Surely you can take two, Miss Evans?'

'Two girls, perhaps. Not a boy and a girl, I'm afraid. I've only the one room, see, and my brother's particular.'

Particular about what, Carrie wondered. But Miss Evans looked nice; a little like a red squirrel Carrie had once seen, peering round a tree in a park. Reddish brown hair and bright, button eyes, and a shy quivering look.

Carrie said, 'Nick sleeps in my room at home because he has bad dreams sometimes. I always look after him and he's no trouble at all.'

Miss Evans looked doubtful. 'Well, I don't know what my brother will say. Perhaps I can chance it.' She smiled at Carrie.

'The strongest memory is weaker than the palest ink'

Recollections of real-life experience can be gleaned from children's relatives or older members of the local community, as in the following example.

I was born on 7th March 1920. There was just mum and dad and my brother, Bert, who was 8 years older and we were a loving and close-knit family. My grandparents lived a few streets away and every Sunday the whole family, including my aunt and cousins, would go round for dinner. We often had rabbit stew – I can smell it now – with home-made bread to dip in. My grandad wore a striped shirt with a stiff collar and always a waistcoat. He had a big moustache and whenever he went out he would wear his bowler hat.

After dinner, the grown ups would be in the living room, knocking back grandad's assortment of home-made wines, while we grandchildren played in the front room. Before we left, grandma would bring out her surprise tin for us children.

My father was a railwayman who had 60 poles of allotment overlooking the railway line. When he was on the right shift he would take me with him. There was a large hut at the top of the garden field, and we would sit on the form outside, watching the trains go by. He knew every one and, without fail, his pocket watch with a long silver chain would come out to see if they were late.

Katherine's great grandma

Why the Agouti Has No Tail

Remembrance, of course, is not confined to comparatively recent memories. The story-teller has, for centuries, ensured cultural continuity by passing on traditional tales from generation to generation. Popular collections, comprising stories from around the world are contained in Time for Telling, The Big-Wide-Mouthed-Toad-Frog *and* The King with Dirty Feet, *by Mary Medlicott, Letterbox Library.*

Another splendid collection of traditional stories from around the world is Why the Agouti has no tail, and other stories *by Floella Benjamin, Hutchinson 1984, From which the next story comes.*

An agouti is a small animal that lives in the West Indies. It looks something like a squirrel, only it doesn't have a tail. A long time ago, however, the agouti did have a fine tail and this is the story of how it lost it.

Once upon a time the dog and the agouti were very good friends and lived together happily. One day Agouti and Dog were lazing in the garden, enjoying the afternoon sun when along came Goat, who was looking very pleased with himself.

'What are you so happy about?' asked Dog.

'I've been invited to a party,' replied Goat with satisfaction.

Now, both Dog and Agouti loved parties and when they heard this their ears pricked up.

'What party is this?' said Agouti. 'We want to come as well.'

'Oh, you can't come,' said Goat haughtily. 'This party is only for animals which have horns.' Then he trotted off with his head in the air.

Dog and Agouti looked at each other. Neither of them had horns and that meant that they would definitely not be going to the party.

'Oh, dear,' said Dog. 'I do love parties; there is always lots of food to eat.'

'This has spoilt my whole day,' said Agouti, and he went indoors to sulk.

The next day Dog and Agouti went into town. The news of the party had spread and everyone was talking about it, especially the animals with horns. Apparently, the party was to be held on a small island some distance away. There was to be a barbecue and lots of rum-punch to drink. All the horned animals were to leave for the island, by boat, the next morning and return in the evening after the party.

'It's not fair.' said Dog. 'I must find a way to go to the party.'

'But you don't have horns,' said Agouti. 'You would soon be spotted and then there would be trouble.'

'Don't worry, I will find a way,' said Dog, and he disappeared into the forest, leaving his friend Agouti behind.

Dog walked along a narrow path which led through the trees. He just had to think of a way to get invited to the party, but however hard he thought, he couldn't come up with any ideas.

Suddenly, as he rounded a corner, he saw a pile of old bones in front of him on the path. They were the remains of a cow that had died many years ago.

What luck, thought Dog, as he spotted a lovely pair of horns amongst the pile of bones. He picked them up and tied them to his head with a strong piece of vine. Then he rushed home to show his friend Agouti.

But Agouti was not very pleased when he saw Dog with the horns. 'It's all right for you. You are large enough to pass as a horned animal. But what about me? I would soon be spotted. There are no horned animals as small as I am. I still can't go to the party.' Agouti was more miserable than ever and he sat in a corner and sulked.

The next morning Dog was up bright and early. He tied the horns to his head as tightly as he could. 'Come down to the jetty with me, Agouti,' he pleaded, 'and see if my disguise works.'

Reluctantly, Agouti agreed. He was interested to see if Dog could get away with the deception.

The jetty was bustling with horned animals, all waiting for the boat to arrive and take them across to the island. So none of them noticed as Dog, wearing his horns, slipped quietly amongst them.

Agouti watched as Dog climbed aboard the boat and sat down next to Goat. His heart beat faster, as he realised that his best friend was going to get away with the trick and go to the party without him. He was so jealous that, before he could stop himself, he cried out. 'Stop! Stop! There is an imposter aboard.'

At this, all the horned animals looked at Dog and saw that he had tricked them. They picked him up angrily and threw him into the water.

When Agouti realised what his jealous betrayal had done, he turned and ran as fast as he could, with Dog close on his heels. He ran and ran as fast as his short legs could carry him, but Dog was angry and humiliated and soon caught up with Agouti, who scurried into a nearby hole. But Agouti wasn't quite fast enough, and Dog snapped off his tail as he disappeared down the hole.

Well, needless to say, Dog and Agouti were no longer friends, and if you are ever in the West Indies and you see a dog scratching and barking at a hole, it is probably because there is an agouti down there. That is how the agouti lost its tail.

The story can be used as the basis for discussion about different cultures, and how people adjust to them. The theme can be explored further through *When Africa was Home* by Karen Lynn Williams, and *Grace and Family*, the sequel to Mary Hoffman's widely-acclaimed *Amazing Grace*, (Letterbox Library).

The way we were

As the home lives of many children today are somewhat complicated, it may be considered unwise to pursue such time-honoured investigations into family background and continuity as the family tree. However, artefacts such as medals, photographs, jewellery, certificates, ornaments etc. can evoke strong memories and provide useful starting points for class projects.

Tinned pineapple

The drawer full of old photographs was the best thing about visiting Grandma's. I rushed straight into the front room, pulled the middle drawer from the polished wooden cabinet and lay comfortably on the rug shuffling the photographs between my fingers. My favourites were the brown and white ones, stuck to card, stiff like their subjects. Edwardian girls, unsmiling, hair pulled back severely from the forehead and pinned, waists pinched, blouses starched, feet swallowed by tightly laced boots.

Were they the perfect children they seemed? Did they ever unpin their hair and let it blow untidily in the breeze, unlace those boots and dangle toes in water ... or answer back their mothers?

One girl was positively scowling. On the back, scrawled in pencil, Granny Lou 1910. My Great Grandma. 'Must be who I get my bad temper from' I thought.

That was the real reason I was at Grandma's. This room offered sanctuary. A quiet, undisturbed haven where I could escape the arguments and quarrels that lately seemed daily occurrences at home. Recently, nothing I did seemed right. According to Mum I was 'lazy, unhelpful, moody, resentful, argumentative, thoughtless, noisy, disrespectful' mostly all at the same time. There was a pattern to our rows. Prolonged silences, criticism from Mum followed by spectacular outbursts of temper from me. The volley of angry words fired from my mouth left their marks on Mum's face, which seemed to age with every exchange. Slamming the door behind me, I would charge into the garden, but by the time I reached the gate I was already sorry.

'Wasn't he handsome in his uniform then?' Gran leaned over my shoulder and pointed to the young man in naval uniform, his unlined face smiling proudly at the photographer. 'This was taken when he'd just been made up to Chief Petty Officer' she said. I knew what was coming.

'He came home on leave from Chatham where he was in charge of the stores. His suitcase was so heavy he had a job to walk upright when he came into the house. He set it down where you're sitting now, lifted the lid and well, I didn't know whether to laugh or cry. I felt sure he'd get into trouble but he just smiled and said.

'Get the tin opener, girl, we'll have a feast.'

The case was full of tinned fruit. Big catering tins like they use in canteens. Pears, peaches, oranges, but best of all pineapples.

We hadn't seen a pineapple for years …

'Gran, who's this?' I interrupted. I wasn't in the mood for her stories, so I held a black and white photo in front of her face.

'You ought to know what that is. It's your mum. Taken in the front garden where Grandad's cutting the hedge.'

I remembered the Chief Petty Officer, strands of hair spread over his pink scalp, standing precariously on a stepladder, snipping at the privet with oversized shears, the ageless warm smile greeting me as I'd raced up the path earlier that afternoon.

'She was about your age then. Wearing her new school uniform, you see. There's her satchel lying on the grass.'

I hadn't realised how alike we looked.

I told Gran, 'She looks just like me.'

'Yes, but looks can deceive. She was nothing like you at all, you know. She was a right madam, your mother. Couldn't ever do anything right for her when she was that age. We could hardly be in the same room for five minutes, but there was a row. Then she'd fly off the handle at the least little thing. Grandad used to say, 'She'd made a saint swear.' You knew when it was coming. She'd look as miserable as sin. What I called – Granny Lou face.'

Remembering the sepia scowl, I nodded sympathetically.

'She'd have her say, slam the door and be gone before we could stop her. It upset me more than she knew. I used to come in here and have a little weep. Then, later on, she'd creep back as nice as pie as if nothing had happened. Not a bit like you really. Now that's a surprise, isn't it?'

I didn't answer. Instead I put the photographs back in the drawer. Except for one. That one I slipped into my pocket.

'Can I stay for tea, Gran?' I asked.

'Of course you can. What would you like to eat?' she replied kindly.

'I don't suppose you have any tinned pineapple, have you?'

Ian Addis

Bereavement and loss

The highly sensitive subject of bereavement and loss, be it through the death of a relative, friend or even a pet, can often prove difficult to address in school. The careful use of story often helps children come to terms with grief by depersonalising the issue, enabling a shared response which may offer comfort.

ADDITIONAL RESOURCES:

Badger's Parting Gifts, Susan Varley, Picture Lions
Come back Grandma, Sue Limb, The Bodley Head

Goodbye Mitch, Ruth Wallace-Brodens, Letterbox Library
The Tenth Good Thing About Barney, Judith Voirst, Collins
Conker, Michael Morpurgo, Heinemann
Goodnight Mister Tom, Michelle Magorian, Kestrel
Water Bugs and Dragonflies, Doris Stickney, Mowbray
Ben's Flowers, What can the matter be, and other stories, David Fulton Publishers
An extensive booklist on children and bereavement can be obtained from:
Cruse – Bereavement Care, 126 Sheen Road, Richmond, Surrey, TW9 1UR,
and a further useful resource for teachers is: *Coping with Bereavement: A Handbook for Teachers,* John Holland, 1996, Cardiff Academic Press, St Fagan's Road, Fairwate, Cardiff CF5 3AE.
Helpful advice on coping with crises in school, in the light of such tragic events as the *Herald of Free Enterprise* disaster, Hillsborough and Dunblane, can be found in the booklet, *Wise before the event*, by William Yule and Anne Gold, Calouste Gulbenkian Foundation.

Religious festivals of remembrance

On All Souls Day, celebrated on 2 November, the **Christian** Church remembers all those who have died. Flowers are taken to cemeteries or crematoria, and the names of the dead may be read out in church.

At the Feast of Obon, Japanese **Buddhists** light lanterns and prepare food for the visit of departed ancestors, while on the Chinese All Souls Day, Buddhists visit the temple and ceremoniously burn a large paper boat to help wandering spirits across the 'sea of want, hunger, thirst and torment'.

During the autumn festival of Yom Kippur, **Jews** hold a special memorial service for those who have died, and worshippers are urged to remember the happy times shared when they were alive. Mourners pledge to give Tzedekah, a gift to charity, in memory of their loved ones.

Cross-curricular links

The most accessible resource for investigative work on continuity in the community is likely to be the local church which may harbour a wealth of architectural features, artefacts and stories which can stimulate work in many areas of the curriculum. Most churches also have a story associated with them, and one such is the story of St Swithun. He is associated with Winchester cathedral.

The original shrine of Saint Swithun was destroyed in 1538, and a modern canopy covers the spot where it is thought to have stood.

The story of Saint Swithun

Swithun was a powerful and well-known figure in the early Christian Church during the eighth century. He had joined the monastery at Winchester, eventually becoming Abbot and Bishop, and many stories are told of his kindness and wisdom.

One day, a woman was crossing a narrow bridge over a river, on her way to market. She was carrying eggs in her apron, which she hoped to sell, but was so badly jostled and pushed by the

---

crowd that they fell to the ground and were broken. Swithun happened to be passing at the time, saw the rough way in which she had been treated, and stooped to retrieve the eggs. When she looked at them, they were all unbroken and she was able to sell them in the market as she had intended.

On his death in 862, Swithun was buried, at his own request, in a simple grave outside the walls of the cathedral. He believed that the sky made a better roof than any tomb carved from stone.

When the cathedral was rebuilt during the reign of William the Conqueror, it was decided that such an important saint should have a more impressive resting place and plans were made to rebury Swithun in a new tomb inside the building. Work began on 15 July 1077, but so did torrential rain, which persisted for forty days, frustrating all attempts to move the grave. This was interpreted as evidence that the saint wished to remain buried in the original place, so a little chapel was built over the grave instead, and many pilgrims came to worship at the shrine.

After events on that first St Swithun's day, people have predicted that rain on 15 July will herald forty days of similar weather.

In keeping with the legend, one side of the modern canopy is grey and decorated with raindrops while the other depicts golden sunshine.

Activities

Many of the themes outlined above can be extended through class, year group, Key Stage or whole school activities.

Interpretations of history

The National Curriculum Key Stage 2 history programme of study requires that pupils examine the impact of the Second World War on the people of Britain. Displays of artefacts, collections of anecdotal accounts, photographs, etc. can involve children in accumulating evidence, and increase their understanding.

Studying an aspect of local history might well include a town or village study, incorporating visits to places of historical significance. The local church building invariably offers a readily available resource, while additional information can be gleaned from gravestones, church records, war memorials and interviews with older members of the community.

Historical enquiry

At both Key Stages 1 and 2, pupils are required to find out about aspects of the past from a range of sources of information, including artefacts, pictures and photographs, adults talking about their past, written sources and buildings and sites.

Sketching unusual artefacts or utensils can heighten a child's understanding of their original purpose.

Role-play, in which pupils re-enact the lives of Victorian schoolchildren, is an effective method of enhancing identification with the times.

The use of comparative photographs of the locality, illustrating changes in land use, roads, building development, methods of transport, costume etc. can be an effective method of highlighting 'differences between ways of life at different times'.

Three-dimensional maps of the area can be compiled, using the photographs, to reflect the changes.

Children can compile a class time-line, including key events in their lifetime, supported by personal evidence such as baby photos, newspaper cuttings, school achievements etc.

ADDITIONAL RESOURCES:

A resource pack called *Working People 1900–1950* is available from SCIP (Schools/Industry Partnership), Centre for Industry and Education, University of Warwick, Coventry CV4 7AL.
A Teacher's Guide to Using Historic Houses, Gail Durbin, English Heritage 1993.
This and other useful resource material to support using the historic environment as part of programmes of study across many curriculum subjects is detailed in a catalogue available from: English Heritage Education Service, 429 Oxford Street, London, W1R 2HD (0171 973 3442 / 3443).

Diaries

Such famous publications as Samuel Pepys' diary and the day-to-day observations of Anne Frank, provide unique insight into the past.
Children can be encouraged to record their own thoughts over a period of time, reflecting upon happenings at school and at home. In addition to factual observations, their records might contain references to their feelings, hopes and fears.

Spiritual and cultural awareness

The wide-ranging theme of remembrance offers a wealth of opportunities for children to increase their spiritual and cultural development.

Contemplative, quiet times during the school assembly can be enhanced by listening to appropriate music or poetry, especially when addressing emotional issues such as bereavement and grief. At such times, class activities which enable pupils to express their feelings in writing and discussion, or through role-play, are valuable in creating a safe, secure environment, sensitive to individual needs.

(Activities detailed in *Sharing Nature with Children* by JB Cornell, Deep Books 1994, explore life-cycles in the natural world, widening children's understanding of the process of continuity.)

Chapter 6

Ring out Wild Bells

$\mathbf{F}$or many schools, the celebration of Christmas places immense pressure on an already over-loaded curriculum. It is difficult to justify spending a disproportionate amount of time on traditional activities. Yet, with careful planning, the festival can form an integral part of a well-balanced, cross-curricular topic, enjoyed by the whole school.

Historical background to Christmas

The choice of 25 December as the **birthday of Jesus** was arbitrary, but hardly random. The date almost coincides with the **Winter Solstice** (22/23 December) which is the shortest day of the year in the Northern Hemisphere. This was a time when the ancient pagans rejoiced, anticipating longer daylight hours, warmer weather and the re-awakening of the natural world.

Christian customs originating from this festivity are the decorative use of evergreens, the leaves symbolising the renewal of life, and the lighting of the Yule log. The great log was brought into the house, lit from the remains of the previous year's fire, to burn throughout the twelve days of the festive period.

The **Romans** devoted 25 December to the 'Feast of the Unconquered Sun', but it was from their festival of Saturnalia, held in honour of the god of seed-corn, that the modern Christmas customs of present-giving and parties are derived.

Christmas-tide begins with **Advent**, which also marks the start of the Christian year.

This occurs on the fourth Sunday before Christmas, and is the traditional time for preparations for the festival to begin. (Ideas for Advent calendars are detailed later in this section, while reference to Advent candles occurs on page 86.)

St Nicholas Day is celebrated on 6 December and commemorates the life and work of the Bishop of Myra, in Asia Minor, who died on that day circa AD 320. Many stories are told about the popular bishop, most demonstrating his renowned kindness and generosity.

St Nicholas has become recognised as the patron saint of children and, in many parts of the world, youngsters receive their Christmas presents on the eve of his festival. St Nicholas was also popular with seafaring people, and when Dutch families migrated from the Netherlands to begin new lives in North America during the seventeenth century, they took their saint with them. Sinterklass, as he was known, became Santa Claus. Eventually the practice of giving presents travelled back across the Atlantic Ocean, becoming established in Britain as a Christmas Eve tradition.

In **Sweden**, the Christmas season begins on 13 December when **St Lucia**, the queen of light, is commemorated. Young daughters of the household, dressed in white and wearing a crown of greenery decorated with candles, treat the rest of the family to a breakfast of coffee and freshly-baked Lucia buns. Candle-lit processions around neighbouring homes take place and Christmas preparations begin.

The first religious service of Christmas is the Midnight Mass on **Christmas Eve**, although many churches hold family services to enable children to attend. A common feature is the Christmas crib depicting the scene at the stable in Bethlehem with the baby Jesus in a manger surrounded by the figures of Mary, Joseph, the shepherds and the wise men.

St Francis of Assisi is often credited with the popularisation of the Christmas crib, and may have introduced the familiar animals, the ox and the ass, into the tableau.

The occasion may take the form of a **Christingle service**. After carol singing and readings from the Christmas story, all the children are given an orange with a little candle placed on top, and small cocktail sticks each bearing nuts, sweets or raisins, and with a red ribbon tied around. The orange symbolises the world, the candle represents Jesus, the light of the world, the nuts, sweets and raisins remind us of the fruits of the world, and the red ribbon signifies the blood of Christ and His sacrifice on the cross.

Christmas Day is the centrepiece of the festival. At church services, Christian worshippers receive the Christmas communion, kneeling before the altar to take bread and wine, acknowledging both the occasion of Christ's birth, and His death on the cross and ultimate resurrection. Changing lifestyles may have altered people's attitudes to the traditional Christmas but the special dinner of roast turkey and plum pudding remains a highlight for many families.

December 26 is known as **St Stephen's Day** or **Boxing Day**. St Stephen was an early Christian martyr, stoned to death for his faith. He is particularly honoured by having his special day immediately after Christ's birthday.

Boxing Day reminds us of the medieval custom of opening the 'poor boxes', which were kept in churches and into which donations were placed throughout the year. The proceeds were distributed to the needy of the parish. This tradition led to the practice of giving gifts to servants and apprentices in the form of money in a small box, and it is still common to reward regular visitors (like the paper-boy, postman or milkman) with a 'Christmas box'.

Symbols of Christmas

Many traditional Christmas artefacts have their origins in Victorian times.

The **Christmas tree** was introduced into Britain by Queen Victoria's husband, Albert Prince Consort, in 1841.

Christmas cards originate from a prototype designed in 1843 by the artist J C Horsley. A thousand cards, decorated with a seasonal illustration and the caption 'A merry Christmas and a happy New Year to you', were printed and sold for one shilling (5p) each. The idea caught on, and by 1880, when publisher Sir Adolph Tuck arranged a competition to promote original designs, the production of cards was already a commercial reality.

The **Christmas cracker** owes its invention to the creative imagination and business acumen of a London confectioner, Tom Smith.

Holly has been a symbol of friendship and love since pagan times. In the familiar carol 'The Holly and the Ivy', its prickly, evergreen leaves and red berries are linked to features of the ivy plant, and this image is associated with the birth, life and death of Christ.

Mistletoe has a similar association with eternal love, derived from the ancient Norse legend of Baldur. Loki used the plant to kill his rival, but on Baldur's return to life it was promised that mistletoe would never cause harm again.

Twelfth night, 6 January, or the Feast of Epiphany (from the Greek word meaning 'appearance') marks the occasion of the visit of the three kings, wise men or Magi, to the Infant Jesus. 'Magi' was the name given to early astronomers, and would account for their famous journey 'following a star'. Their gifts – gold, frankincense and myrrh – symbolise royalty, divinity and death. Gold was rare, durable and beautiful, frankincense burned at religious ceremonies and myrrh was used in the embalming and preservation of the dead.

Today, Twelfth Night is the time to take down our decorations, but in olden times the 'official' end of Christmas was celebrated by a huge feast. One custom was to place a dried pea or bean inside a cake, called the Twelfth Cake. Whoever received the slice containing the pea or bean became king or queen of the festivities for the night.

Further information and resources can be found in *Festive Occasions in the Primary School*, by Redvers Brandling, Ward Lock 1978.

There is an abundance of Christmas literature, and useful anthologies containing examples of the best material are *The Oxford Book of Christmas Stories* (OUP) and *Christmas* (Scholastic Publications Collections Series, 1992). The following selection of stories explores many of the different aspects of Christmas. The story of the nativity is related in the gospels of St Matthew and St Luke, Chapters 1 and 2.

St Nicholas and the bags of gold

Nicholas was a young man who was very kind, very helpful and thoughtful, and very rich. The fact that he was so wealthy worried him because he thought it unfair that he should have so much when he knew there were others in the world who had so little. But what could he do about it? He knew that even if he gave all his money away, there would not be enough to help all the people who needed it.

One night when Nicholas was on his way home he passed a house and heard the sound of crying. He knew that in this house lived a father and his three daughters. He knew that the father had once been a rich merchant, but that he had lost all his money in some foolish buying and selling. He knew that the father worked hard to earn a living, but that it could not have been easy to earn enough money for all four of them.

Nicholas hurried on, but as he passed the door he heard the eldest daughter say, 'I know I have to leave. I know there isn't enough money for us all to live here any more. I know I have to find work as a servant or a slave, but I'm frightened. I don't know where to go or what to do.' He heard her youngest sister say to her father 'Can't she stay? Does she have to leave?' And he heard the father reply 'There is no choice. We cannot all continue to live here in this house. You must each find work where you can. There is no hope here in this house. You must all leave.'

Nicholas heard the dejection in the man's voice and knew it was not what he wanted for his daughters. He heard the eldest daughter start to cry again.

Nicholas hurried away from the house, planning how he could help the family. He had money, they needed money. It was simple, he would give them help in such a way that they would not know it was him.

Later, much later that night, Nicholas returned to the house, There was no-one about. There was no light showing from inside the house. Everyone must be asleep. Nicholas crept round to the back of the house. There was a low wall there and Nicholas climbed on to it. From here he could climb on to the roof. Carefully, quietly, stealthily, always looking around to see that no-one had seen him, Nicholas edged his way along the roof tiles towards the chimney. He held tightly to the chimney stack with one hand and felt in his pocket with the other. He pulled out the heavy, cloth bag containing a hundred gold pieces. Enough there to ensure that the eldest girl did not have to leave home.

Nicholas dropped the cloth bag down the chimney. He heard it land in the grate with a dull thud and a chink as the metal pieces settled into the ashes. Nicholas stayed quite still for a few more minutes, checking that the sound had not woken any of the people in the house, but everything stayed quiet. Nicholas carefully climbed down from the roof and went home.

He could only guess at the surprise of the merchant and his daughters the next morning when they found a bag of gold in their fireplace.

The next night Nicholas went back to the house. He had decided that one bag of gold was not enough. There were, after all, three daughters. Surely that meant there should be three bags of gold. He dropped another bag down the family's chimney.

When the merchant discovered the second bag of gold, his surprise of the first day was nothing compared to his astonishment on the second.

'Two bags!' he said. 'Yet I have three daughters ... surely it won't happen again? Tonight I must wait up all night just in case the visitor returns. I must thank him. If it were not for this unknown helper, our family would by now be split up and who knows if we would ever see each other again.'

That night when the girls had gone to bed, their father sat in the corner of the dark living room, watching, waiting, listening. It was hard to stay awake, but in the early hours of the morning, the man heard a sound. A scraping, scrabbling sound like feet on tiles, slipping, sliding. Then silence. Then a rattle and a thud and a chink as a heavy cloth bag came clattering down the chimney.

Quickly as he could the man leaped from his chair, across the room and out of the door, to catch the helper, to thank him and to find out who he was.

But he was too late. The mystery helper was already running down the road, and all the merchant could see was his long red cloak flapping behind him as he ran.

The next day the girls' father searched the town to try to find the man who had helped them, but without success. No-one seemed to know of him, or to have heard of him. Nicholas was nowhere to be found.

Yet, in the days that followed, there were more stories of people who had been helped, but by whom, they didn't know. But each time, the way they had been helped was the same. Gold pieces in cloth bags were dropped down the family chimneys.

Jeanne L Jackson

An interpretation of the journey of the Magi is recounted in the traditional Russian folk-tale of Baboushka. A definitive version can be found in Arthur Scholey's retelling of the tale, Lion Publishing, 1989.

The Christmas Rose

This version of the 'Christmas rose' story has additional emotional charge if a sprig of the plant is produced at the end of the reading.

The journey to town was tiring in the hot summer sun. The children grew restless and began to complain, but their mother soon put an end to their moans.

'It's no good whining,' she said firmly. 'If we don't go to market, we don't sell our wares, and if we don't sell our wares, we starve. It's not much further now. If you're good, I'll take you to see the beautiful monastery garden before we return to the forest.'

Ever since their father had been banished from the town for stealing bread and milk to feed his growing family, they had lived as outcasts, making a poor living picking forest fruits, growing plants and collecting firewood to sell at the market.

The townsfolk shunned the ragged mother and her children as they trudged through the narrow streets, laden with produce. But once they had set up their stall in the market square, the people flocked to buy the plump berries, tender herbs and bunches of bright flowers. When the long day at market finally drew to a close, the children reminded their mother of her promise. She led them to the great stone wall that surrounded the monastery, carefully opened the gate, and went inside.

It was so quiet, so peaceful after the bustle of the market, but the calm was short-lived. One of the gardeners spotted the unwelcome visitors and shouted angrily,

'This is the abbot's private garden. Be off with you now, or I'll put you out!'

Gathering her children around her, the outcast mother looked about her.

'It is truly a wonderful garden,' she said, admiringly. 'But not so wonderful as ours. At the stroke of midnight on Christmas Eve, the flowers of all the seasons grow together at the same time, in celebration of our Saviour's birth. And the most beautiful of all are those with frail silver petals and golden stamens. We call them Christmas roses.'

'Rubbish,' replied the gardener, roughly. 'I know of no such flowers', and he began to drive the intruders towards the gate.

But the old abbot, walking in another part of the garden, had overheard the mother's words. He remembered hearing as a child how part of the great forest was transformed into a magical garden on Christmas Eve, and he hurried to catch the family before they were turned outside.

'Good mother,' he called gently. 'I would dearly love to see your wonderful garden. I am old and I fear this year may be my last. Perhaps one of your children might guide me to the spot on Christmas Eve?'

'Why should I trust you?' replied the outcast. 'You could drive us from our cave if we show you where it is.'

The abbot smiled.

'I would not do that. Rather than wish you harm, I promise to ask the Lord Bishop to grant your husband a pardon and allow you all to come back to town once more in return for your kindness.'

The mother paused thoughtfully.

'Very well,' she said, 'but you must give me your word that the only people to accompany you into the forest will be my eldest son and this gardener.'

The abbot agreed, and when the family had left, he approached the Lord Bishop with the story of the miraculous garden. The bishop promised to grant the abbot's request, provided he brought back one of the silver and gold flowers to plant in the monastery grounds.

When Christmas Eve arrived, the old abbot and his gardener set off together into the wintry night. The outcasts' eldest son was waiting at the edge of the forest, as arranged. The three plodded on through the snow, deeper and deeper into the dense undergrowth, until they reached the cave, where a bright fire beckoned cheerfully.

'Sit down and warm yourselves,' said the outcast mother as the travellers entered. 'Sleep if you can. I'll wake you when it is time.'

The old abbot, exhausted from his journey, slept peacefully until he was woken by the sound of church bells, heralding the arrival of Christmas Day. Then, as the ringing stopped, the icy wind died away. Instead he felt a warm, gentle breeze which wafted through the cave. Outside, the sky lightened, the snow melted and a glorious array of bright flowers sprang up from the green earth. The outcast parents looked on proudly as their happy children played on the grass. And, on noticing the silver and gold flowers sparkling at their feet, the abbot smiled joyfully. Kneeling, he thanked God for allowing him to see such a miracle.

The gardener, however, frightened by the sudden transformation, could not believe it was holy work.

'This is no miracle,' he shouted. 'This is witchcraft and the devil's doing.'

With his words, the sky blackened and the icy wind returned. Snow began to fall and the children ran shivering back into the cave. The abbot staggered forwards, clutching at the earth as he fell. The garden had vanished as quickly as it had appeared, leaving the forest as dark and forbidding as before.

Fearfully, the gardener carried the old man back to the monastery and laid him gently on his bed to rest. But the abbot was gravely ill and, before daybreak, he was dead.

When the other monks saw their master, they marvelled at the radiant smile on his lips, and discovered, clutched tightly in one hand, the root of a strange plant. Overcome with grief and guilt, the gardener planted it lovingly in the abbot's garden and vowed to tend it daily. Time passed, but although there were green leaves there was no sign of a flower. Spring became summer, summer turned to autumn, but still no bud could be seen. The gardener wondered if the plant would ever bloom.

Finally, on Christmas morning, when the monastery garden was sprinkled with snow, the gardener saw a beautiful cluster of the silvery petals and golden stamens pointing towards the sky. He picked a single stem and hurried to tell the bishop his news.

'The abbot kept his promise and I shall keep mine,' the bishop said. 'You can carry the pardon to the outcast family in the forest, and welcome them back into our community once more. Take that flower, the Christmas rose, as a true symbol of our love.'

(Adapted from a Scandinavian legend)

Marcus Pfister's popular story of *The Rainbow Fish* (North South Books) which examines aspects of present-giving, can be easily adapted for a Christmas production and extracts from Charles Dickens' enduring morality tale, *A Christmas Carol*, also offer many opportunities for dramatisation.

Activities

Advent

The practice of making individual Advent calendars provides a useful design technology activity.

1. Enlarge the design from a Christmas card – older children can construct a grid to enable proportionate magnification.

2. Mark and cut openings for 24 boxes of varying shapes and sizes for windows.

3. Number them from 1 to 24.

4. Mount onto backing paper.

5. Open the windows carefully and illustrate behind them.

A large class or school calendar can be used to reinforce good work and behaviour, by allowing children, in turn, to open a daily 'window of recognition', receiving a small prize in return.

Christmas cards

The design and construction of cards is a well established practice and involves a wide variety of techniques. One such example, based on a star shape and constructed with compasses, allows individuality within a structured approach:

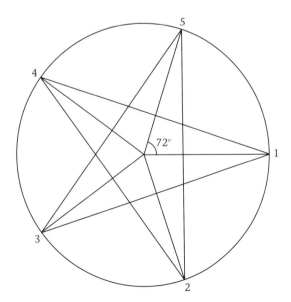

Constructing the 5-pointed star.

1 Draw a circle.

2 Draw in radius 1.

3 Construct angle of 72° at centre.

4 Draw in remaining radii and number 1-5.

5 Join 1 to 3, 3 to 5, 5 to 2, and 2 to 4.

Now trace the outline and decide on a colour scheme. Use coloured foil to complete the pattern.

Postbox

The use of the school 'postbox' can offer a number of opportunities. A rota of postmen, perhaps dressed in seasonal costume, can sort and deliver the cards. Special stamps, designed by the children, can be reproduced on rubber pads and used to frank envelopes. These can then be purchased, raising funds for an identified 'good cause'.

Wrapping paper

Designing wrapping paper can be extended into a productive, purposeful design technology exercise, such as making a bag to contain a present. This involves a range of skills – with regard to shape, size, method of securing etc.

Greenery

Holly, ivy, etc., collected for decorative purposes such as making wreaths or brightening window sills, will offer useful leaf shapes for Christmas motifs. Sheets can be printed from an original design which is cut from card, wood or lino, or individual shapes can be repeated from a template. The motifs might also provide a design for 'ex-libris' stickers given as presents with books or tokens.

Nativity scenes

The construction of nativity scenes for class or school displays provides an opportunity for group activity. Free-standing figures can be made from simple pieces of hessian, cut in conical shapes, soaked in cold water paste and then dressed in biblical fashion.

Decorations

There is no shortage of Christmas craft books giving ideas for decorations such as the 'icosahedron', which incorporates a range of geometric skills.
1. Cut out 20 circles.
2. Fold each circle around an equilateral triangle, leaving flaps of equal size.
3. Open out and colour each circle.
4. Stick a row of ten circles by the flaps – the paste must go right to the edges and the whole flap must be glued. Bend round and finally glue the first to the last.
5. Stick five circles in a ring, forming a peak in the centre.
6. Repeat this with the remaining five circles.
7. Stick one cluster of five on the top of the centre ring and the other on the bottom.

Planning the class party

There are opportunities for data handling in this activity; e.g. asking how many packets of crisps, sausages on sticks, etc. are needed; designing seating plans; making and writing invitations to parent helpers, classroom assistants etc.; making party hats, table decorations, serviettes, and designing games and entertainment.

Christmas lists

Besides the obvious lists of personal presents, children might consider the kind of gifts which would be useful to disabled or handicapped members of society. A mail order catalogue would provide an excellent, free source of material for costing presents and devising practical mathematical tasks.

The Christmas story

Individual books in which the Christmas story unfolds in words and pictures provide children with a delightful resource in the build-up to the end of term.

Modern versions of the nativity

Older children can retell the story in a present-day setting, dramatising it if required.

Copies of famous paintings

Famous paintings can offer stimulating interpretations of the traditional story.

The Christmas service

It is traditional in many schools to hold a service re-enacting the Christmas story through readings, poems and carols. The tableau is the simplest and most effective format. As each part of the story is related, costumed children (usually from the youngest classes) process to the front of the hall, and the nativity scene gradually builds up.

For schools wishing to perform more spectacular productions, composer Peter Canwell has produced several excellent Christmas cantatas: *A Centurion in Bethlehem*, *The Bell that cried*, *The Christmas Dove and the Woodcutter*, and *The First Christmas Rose* are available from IMP, Southend Road, Woodford Green, Essex IG8 8HN.

Chapter 7

A Bright New Morning

Apart from being a new date in the calendar, the New Year has little real significance and most major faiths recognise a different New Year's Day from that which is celebrated in Britain. The **Gregorian calendar**, introduced by Pope Gregory in 1582, to replace the original Julian version, was not officially accepted by the British parliament until 170 years later. By that time, Britain had fallen 11 days behind the countries which had adopted it earlier. When the change took place, the days between the 2 and 14 September were dropped, causing riots in the streets by people who thought their lives were being shortened by 11 days.

This **solar calendar** is based on the number of days taken by the Earth to orbit the Sun. Jews, Buddhists, Muslims, Hindus and Sikhs follow a **lunar calendar** (the 12 months of their year begin at the time of each new moon) the year being 11 days shorter than its 365 day solar counterpart.

The **Christian** Church's year commences with Advent, four weeks before Christmas (see Chapter 6).

Jews celebrate the festival of **Rosh Hashanah** (the first day of the year) in September or October. On Rosh Hashanah God seats Himself on His throne, the record of all human lives is opened, and all the secret thoughts and hidden acts of every person are revealed. Loud blasts are sounded on a shofar (ram's horn), and every human being pauses before God, who decrees the destiny of each one. However, by sincerely repenting of wrongdoing, by devotion to prayer and by performing acts of kindness, it is possible for people to change the course of their lives.

Over the period of the festival, a shofar is blown in the synagogue, the rabbi wears a white robe and the scrolls of the Torah are covered in white. In the home at this time it is customary to place honey on the table at meals. Each person dips a piece of apple and hallah bread into the honey and says the following words:

> *May it be your will, O God, to give us a good and sweet year.*

Some families practise the custom of **Tashlich** and gather by the banks of a river or lake to recite prayers of forgiveness. After the prayers, the dust and bits of fluff that gather in pockets are shaken out, or breadcrumbs are thrown into the water, to symbolise the casting off of sins before making a new beginning with the approach of the New Year.

In preparation for the **Buddhist** New Year (Losar), it is a custom in some countries for people to clean their houses thoroughly and perform rituals to drive out evil spirits. Then the year begins with three days of merrymaking followed by a similar period of contemplation during the Great Prayer week.

Muslims celebrate the New Year by commemorating the establishment of the first Islamic state at Medina in AD 622. The Islamic year is followed by the letters AH (representing Al-Hijrah, or migration). This recalls Muhammad's journey from Makkah to the new location.

The **Sikh** New Year festival, **Baisakhi**, is celebrated in April and commemorates the initiation of the first Amrit ceremony by Guru Gobind Singh, the tenth Guru (see Chapter 2).

Important artefacts known as **the five Ks**, originally presented to the five Sikhs who offered themselves in sacrifice to the tenth Guru, are worn. These are:

1. the kirpan – a sword to defend the good and the poor;
2. the kara – a bracelet to remind Sikhs of God's love;
3. the kangha – a comb to keep the hair tidy;
4. the kesh – uncut hair;
5. the kachera – shorts.

The tradition on this day is to renew the Nishan Sahib, the Sikh flag, which flies from each gurdwara. The flagpost is taken down, the chola, or flagcloth, removed, the post is washed and a new chola affixed. The Amrit ceremony is then performed, and followed by a range of activities including sports, martial arts, music and poetry competitions.

The Chinese calendar names each lunar year, cyclically, after an animal – the rat, ox, tiger, rabbit, dragon, snake, horse, sheep, monkey, cock, dog and pig (see also 'The Chinese New Year' below).

ADDITIONAL RESOURCES:

Celebrations, Jane Cooper, Wayland
Faiths and Festivals, Martin Palmer, Ward Lock

A bright new morning

The start of the New Year provides each school with an opportunity to re-evaluate its ethos, requiring that members assess their own lives and values. The theme of working towards a 'bright new morning', in the context of the individual, the school and the wider community, is central to this chapter.

One Day

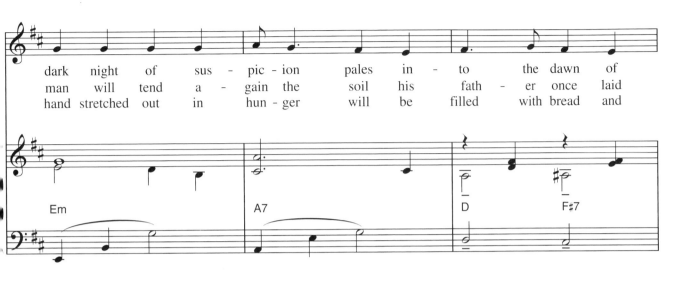

dark night of sus - pic - ion pales in - to the dawn of
man will tend a - gain the soil his fath - er once laid
hand stretched out in hun - ger will be filled with bread and

Em   A7   D   F#7

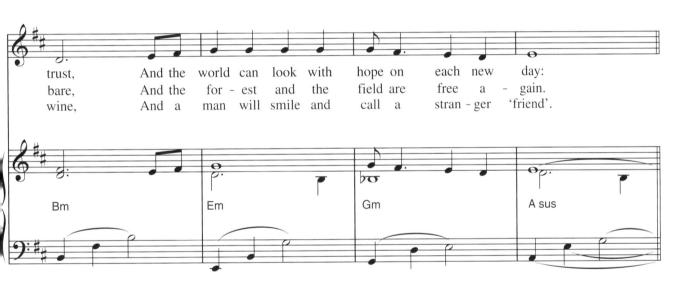

trust,   And the world can look with hope on each new day:
bare,   And the for - est and the field are free a - gain.
wine,   And a man will smile and call a stran - ger 'friend'.

Bm   Em   Gm   A sus

CHORUS

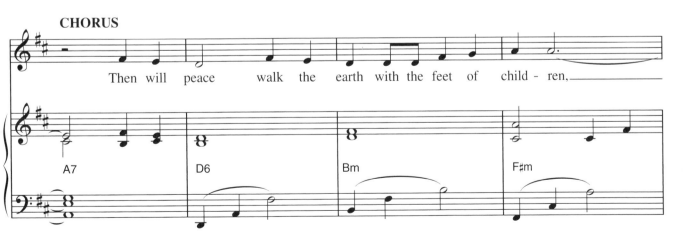

Then will peace walk the earth with the feet of child - ren,_____

A7   D6   Bm   F#m

And will love join the child-ren hand in hand;

D7 G A7 F#m

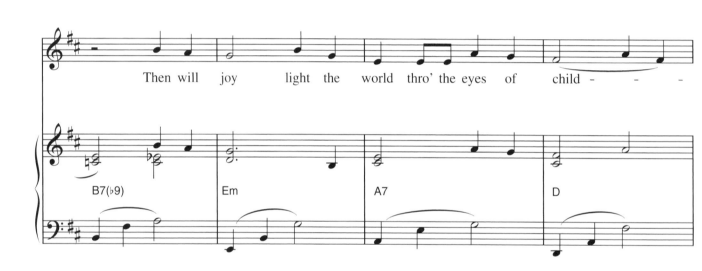

Then will joy light the world thro' the eyes of child - - -

B7(b9) Em A7 D

D.S.

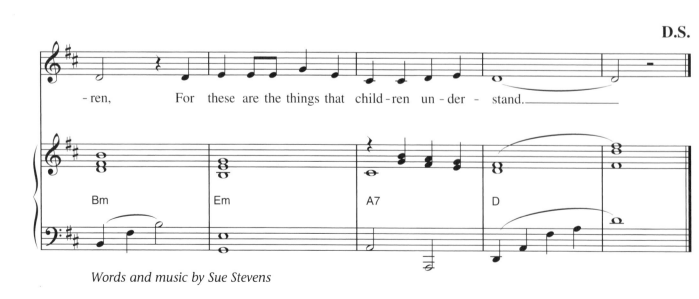

-ren, For these are the things that child-ren un - der - stand._____

Bm Em A7 D

Words and music by Sue Stevens

New Year resolutions

Most people set out in the New Year with good intentions. That people can exercise dramatic change in their own lives and in the lives of others is evidenced by the following inspiring stories of St Paul, Guru Nanak, Prince Siddhartha and Father Damien.

St Paul

Saul was a Roman, and like most of the Romans, Saul hated the Christians.

He did not believe that Jesus was the Son of God. He did not like the Christians to talk about Jesus and to say what a good man he was. He did not like Jesus' disciples preaching to the people and asking them to become Christians too. He wanted rid of the Christians.

Saul and his friends persecuted the Christians. They went round from house to house in Jerusalem, finding out which people believed in Jesus, then they captured those people and threw them into prison. They did not care if they hurt the Christians, or even if they killed them.

One day Saul heard that there were some Christians living nearby in the city of Damascus.

'We'll go and get them,' he said to his friends. 'We'll capture them and bring them back here and throw them into prison.'

Saul and his friends set off in the morning. They walked, of course, to Damascus and at first all went well. The weather was good, they had food with them to eat, and they talked and laughed and joked amongst themselves on the way. Around mid-day they were thinking of stopping for a picnic, when suddenly a blinding flash of light lit up the sky. Saul fell to the ground, covering his head with his arms, afraid of what was happening.

Then he heard a voice, 'Saul, Saul! Why are you persecuting me?'

Saul looked up but could see nothing. The others, too, looked round, but although they could all hear the voice, no-one could see where it was coming from.

'Who are you?' said Saul.

'I am Jesus,' said the voice. Saul said nothing, but felt even more afraid.

'Go into Damascus,' continued the voice. 'Go into the city and you will be told what to do.' Then the bright light faded and the friends were left standing, puzzled, on the road.

'What is it?'

'What does it mean?'

'Why did it happen?' they asked.

But Saul said 'I can't see. Even with my eyes open, I can't see anything. The light has blinded me. Take me to the city. Lead me there.'

And so the friends led Saul by the hand into the city of Damascus and took him to the house where they were to stay.

'What is to become of me?' asked Saul. 'What is going to happen?' He felt so afraid that he did not leave the house, or eat or drink anything for three days. Saul did not know that God was about to send someone to help him.

Ananias was a Christian living in Damascus at the time. He had heard of Saul and of the way he persecuted the Christians, and he was afraid of him. Ananias felt even more afraid when he had a dream in which God spoke to him.

'Go and find Saul,' said God in the dream. 'You will find him in a house in Straight Street. Go to him and touch his eyes so that he can see again.'

'But he will kill me,' answered Ananias. 'Everyone knows what terrible things he does to the Christians. If he knows I am a Christian he will at the very least throw me into prison.'

'Go,' said God. 'I have chosen Saul to do a special job. He will not harm you. Go.'

So Ananias went to the house on Straight Street and found Saul. He said 'Saul. God has sent me so that you can see again, and so that you can have the gift of his Holy Spirit.' Then Ananias touched Saul's face. Straight away Saul could see again.

'Now I understand,' said Saul. 'Now I understand that Jesus is the Son of God. I don't want to persecute the Christians any more. I want to be a Christian. I want to tell the world that Jesus is the Son of God.' So Saul the persecutor became Paul the Christian who spread Jesus's word and died for his faith.

Jeanne L Jackson

Guru Nanak

Once in India there was a rich and successful merchant called Duni Chand. He had worked all his life and now he lived in great luxury. He was proud of his wealth and liked to show off about it. Every year he held a big banquet to which he invited all the local religious leaders. He hoped that if he pleased them his spirit and the spirits of his family would be better off when they died.

The wise Guru Nanak was passing near the city one year at the time of the feast. When Duni Chand heard he was close by, he sent Guru Nanak an invitation to the feast, which Guru Nanak was glad to accept.

The wise man, Guru Nanak, and the rich man, Duni Chand, sat side by side at the feast.

'This is a most wonderful meal,' said the Guru. 'But tell me, I am new to this city and there is one thing I do not understand. Why is it that there are seven flags on your front door? What do they mean?'

'Why that is easy to answer,' replied the rich man. 'It is a local custom to show how wealthy you are. Each flag represents a thousand silver coins. Everyone who passes by my house looks at my door and sees seven flags and knows that I have stored seven thousand silver coins, and they can see what a very wealthy man I am, and how important I am.'

'Oh,' said Guru Nanak, and he paused for a moment. Duni Chand thought that the Guru looked very impressed. Then the Guru bent down and took from his bag a needle he had been using to sew up sacks. He gave the needle to Duni Chand, saying, 'Please will you keep this needle safe for me and give it to me in the next life.'

Duni Chand looked at the needle. He was very puzzled. How could he return the needle to the Guru in the next life? He couldn't take the needle with him when he died. Then he realised if he couldn't take a needle, then he couldn't take seven thousand silver coins with him either.

He turned again to the Guru. 'I see I have been foolish,' he said. 'What shall I do now?'

'Share your wealth with others,' answered the Guru, 'that's what's important in life, not storing it up in bags.'

And that is what Duni Chand did. He shared his wealth with the poor in the community.

Guru Nanak encouraged the rich to share their wealth with others. Jesus did the same. Once he told a rich young ruler to sell all he had and to give the money to the poor.

Elizabeth Breuilly and Sandra Palmer

Prince Siddhartha

One day Siddhartha heard some dancing girls in the palace talking of how beautiful the trees were in the royal park just outside the palace. So he asked the king for permission to visit the park. The king reluctantly agreed, but only after he had sent his soldiers to make sure that Siddhartha would see nothing sad or unpleasant there.

Then the prince, in his magnificent chariot, rode out into the royal park. The trees and the flowers were beautiful. But by chance, he happened to see an old man. He was amazed, for he had never seen an old person before, and asked who he was.

'Just an old man.' replied his charioteer.

'No one has told me about becoming old,' said Siddhartha. 'Will I become old and wrinkled like that?' Reluctantly, the charioteer said that he would.

I don't want to be old like that,' said the prince. 'Please drive me back to the palace. I must think about this.'

Later on he took another trip. This time he saw a sick man.

'Can anyone become sick?' he asked the charioteer.

'Yes, Sir,' came the sad reply.

'Turn back,' said the prince. 'I did not know that health could turn to sickness.'

On his next trip, he saw a funeral pass by. Startled, he asked, 'Why is that man lying under a white sheet? He does not move and the people are crying.'

'Sir, he is dead,' replied the charioteer.

'Will we all die?' asked the prince.

'Alas, my Lord, yes,' came the reply. 'No one escapes death.'

Siddhartha thought about this for many days, then took one more trip into the park. This time, he saw a holy man who was under a tree. Although he was poor, this man looked happy and contented. Siddhartha said to his charioteer, 'How can he be happy? Doesn't he know that old age, sickness and death come to everyone in this life?'

'He knows,' said the charioteer. 'But there is a way to happiness and it is up to each man to find it.'

That night Siddhartha decided to leave his home and family and search for a way that would end man's suffering. Leaving his riches behind, he put on a simple yellow robe, picked up a begging-bowl and went out into the world. He was 29 years old.

For six years, he went from teacher to teacher trying to find out why there is suffering and unhappiness in the world. At last, he realised that he must find out the answer for himself. He thought long and hard, sitting under a fig tree called the Bodhi tree.

Finally, the answer came to him that people suffer in life because they are selfish. He discovered that the secret of a happy life lay in helping others and loving all living things. From that day forward, he became known as the Buddha (the Awakened One) which means the person who discovered the secret of real happiness.

Even though he died 2,500 years ago, people still remember the Buddha and try to be like him.

Elizabeth Breuilly and Sandra Palmer

The story of Father Damien

Josef de Veuster-Wouters was born in Tremeloo in Belgium in 1840. At the age of nineteen he followed his brother Pamphile into religious orders, taking the name of Damien and studying for the priesthood. In 1861, Pamphile was invited to travel with a group of young priests to Hawaii, but, shortly before he was to due to leave, he contracted typhus and was unable to go. Damien persuaded the head of his order to allow him to take his brother's place, and in November 1863 he set sail on the four month journey to the other side of the world.

In those days, the beautiful Pacific islands, with their reefs, flowers and smiling, happy people held a terrible secret. Many of the islanders were suffering from Ma'i Pake, leprosy, which had been brought unwittingly to Hawaii by Chinese settlers. By 1865 the Government had become so frightened by the rapid growth of the dreaded disease that it decreed that anyone who contracted it should be sent to an isolated peninsula on the island of Molokai in order to contain its spread.

Two months after his arrival in Honolulu, Damien was sent to his very first job in a run-down Mission in Puna on Hawaii Island. He worked hard, building a house and a church, before moving to a similar post in Kohala. It was while on a visit to Wailuku on the island of Maui for the consecration of a new church that he learned of the need for priests at the leper colony. He had witnessed the pain of separation and the suffering experienced by new victims of the disease when they were forced to board the ships bound for Molokai, and he volunteered his services.

On 11 May 1873, he landed on the island. But nothing could have prepared him for the horrors he discovered. Not only were the people terribly disfigured but they had lost all pride and hope of things improving. Everywhere was dirt and neglect. Damien wrote of the effects of the disease.

'Discoloured patches appear on the skin, especially on the cheeks; and the parts lose their feeling. After a time this discolouration covers the entire body; then ulcers begin to open, chiefly at the extremities. The flesh is eaten away, and gives off a fetid odour; even the breath of the leper becomes so foul that the air around is poisoned with it.'

He began to work tirelessly to improve conditions, constantly seeking help and supplies from the Government in Honolulu. Single-handedly, he fulfilled the functions of doctor, law enforcer, farmer and priest, and gradually he won the esteem of the islanders by giving them back their self-respect. As one leprosy victim wrote,

'He overwhelms us with his solicitous care, and he himself builds our houses. When any one of us is ill, he gives him tea, biscuits and sugar; and to the poor he gives clothes. He makes no distinction ...'

But, one evening in 1885, the inevitable happened. Tell-tale symptoms that he had contracted the disease himself began to appear. Even more disturbing to Damien was the lack of charity and concern for his plight shown by his superiors back in Honolulu. Bravely he worked on, helped by sympathetic priests who had heard great things of his achievements on the island.

On 15 April 1889, aged just 49, he finally gave up the struggle and died, and was buried under the pandanus tree where he had slept on his first night on the island. His sacrifice drew world-wide attention to the disease and, following his death, efforts were increased to relieve the suffering of leprosy victims. Forty- six years later his body was returned to Belgium and a state funeral held in commemoration of his life and work.

(Adapted from People who have helped the world: Father Damien, *by Pam Brown, Exley Publications)*

ADDITIONAL RESOURCES:

Go Free or Die, Jeri Ferris, First Avenue Edition
Young Harriet Tubman, Ann Benjamin, First Start Biography, Troll Associates
(See also *Young Rosa Parks*, *Young Martin Luther King*)

Father Damien

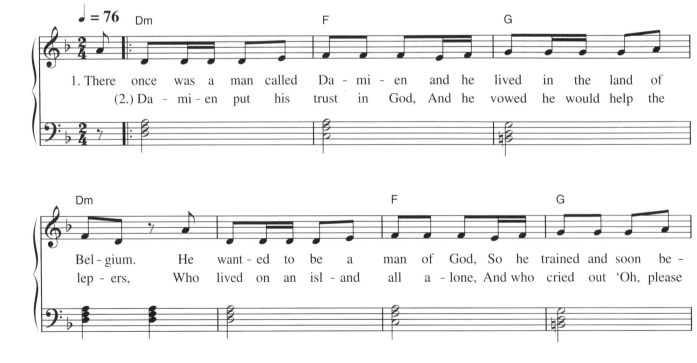

Words and music by Peter Morrell

Poetry for the New Year

Prayer

I said to the man who stood at the gate of the year
Give me a light that I might tread
Safely into the unknown.
And he replied:
'Go out into the darkness and put your hand
Into the hand of God.
That shall be to you better than a light
And safer than a known way.'
So I went forth and finding the hand of God,
Trod gladly into the night.
And He led me towards the hills
And the breaking of day in the lone East.

M. Louise Haskins (1875–1957)

There isn't time

There isn't time, there isn't time
To do the things I want to do
With all the mountain tops to climb
And all the woods to wander through.
And all the seas to sail upon,
And everywhere there is to go
And all the people, everywhere,
Who live upon the earth to know.

Eleanor Farjeon

Celebrations

The arrival of the New Year is celebrated in distinctive style in different parts of the world. One of the most colourful and exciting is the **Chinese New Year**. This is marked by a Spring festival which takes place in late January or February. Celebrations last for several days and end with the 2,000-year-old lantern (Yuanxiao) festival. It is just like Christmas in the West, but it is not a religious holiday.

The legend of the Spring festival

Once upon a time, there was a huge wild animal called Nia. On winter evenings it came to villages or towns to seek food. The people became very frightened as they did not know how to scare the monster away. One day, someone hung a big piece of red cloth in a tall tree to dry. When Nia returned that evening, hunting its prey, it saw the red cloth looming in the sky above and ran away in fear for its life. People were so glad that they had found a way to drive off the monster that they hung red paper on the front door of each house. And since then Nia has never returned.

To commemorate this, the day when Nia ran away forever, the Spring festival is celebrated every year.

The period begins with a symbolic spring-clean, debts are paid and preparations made for a fresh start to the New Year. Houses are decorated with New Year pictures, lanterns are hung, some of which have rotating picture shades, and the doors are hung with red paper strips with poems written on them. The poems consist of two lines, each of which conveys people's hopes for and celebration of the New Year.

Families gather to share a New Year's Eve '**unity dinner**', which often consists of more than ten dishes. New Year's greetings are painted on red paper and displayed on doors, cards are exchanged and the evening ends with a firework display.

People get up early on New Year's morning – especially the children, who find small red envelopes containing sweets or money under their pillows. Everyone is greeted with the familiar 'Kung Hoy Fat Choy' (Happy New Year), which recalls the five blessings of luck, food, long life, health and peace. A favourite delicacy is the New Year's pudding, made of ground glutinous rice, sugar, lard, preserved fruit etc., and glutinous rice dumplings are eaten for breakfast.

During the **Lantern festival**, everywhere is decorated with a variety of different-sized lanterns and there is music and dancing in the streets. One special feature is the dragon dance, when a huge dragon head and body, supported by a team of dancers and to the accompaniment of drums, cymbals and tambourines, weaves its way around the streets collecting money from houses on its route.

Activities

The Chinese New Year

The Chinese New Year story provides a wealth of opportunities for cross-curricular activity. Children can research the fable of how the Chinese years got their names. They can then make masks depicting the 12 animals and re-enact the fable in mime or dance using a series of narrators to retell the story. Familiarity with Chinese music will enable the children to match appropriate instruments and actions to the animals, e. g. maracas for 'scurrying' rats.

Children can compile a chart calculating **the cycle of 'animal' years** over a period. The traditional characteristics of people born during these years are listed below.

The rat – 1984, 1996
People born during the day will have money and an easy life, but if they are born at night they may have to work hard for a living.

The ox – 1985, 1997
These people may have many children, and lead very happy lives.

The tiger – 1986, 1998
These people look after their families very well. The tigress is said to be very clever and cunning.

The rabbit – 1987, 1999
These people love children and lead busy, happy lives.

The dragon – 1988, 2000
These people love night-time, they dislike sudden changes and are short-tempered when their families are attacked.

The snake – 1989, 2001
These people are able to move fast and skilfully. They are wise and strong-minded. They are good at making decisions and they are hardworking.

The horse – 1990, 2002
These are strong, friendly people, especially kind to strangers, but sometimes bad at dealing with 'family'.

The goat – 1991, 2003
These people are born leaders, but also love to help others – they make excellent doctors!

The monkey – 1992, 2004
These people are quick, nimble and very curious. They are loving parents and are rather nosey.

The cockerel – 1993, 2005
These people like to get up early. They are hardworking, and proud and like to decide things for themselves.

The dog –1994, 2006
These people make true, good friends. They are quick thinking and can always be counted on.

The pig – 1995, 2007
These are clever, kind people who make good parents, though they are sometimes short-tempered.

Children might decorate classrooms and other areas around school with red and gold **banners, lanterns** and **fans**.

Other design technology activities could include making the **lucky red envelopes, New Year's cards and scrolls for the two-lined poems**.

The tangram is a traditional form of Chinese picture-making and children will enjoy exploring the variety of subjects possible from the seven basic shapes.

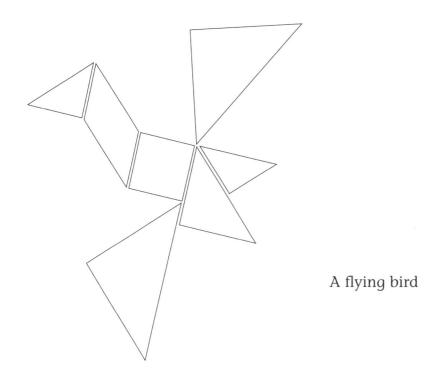

A flying bird

The theme of the New Year can be used to introduce children to other aspects of Chinese culture such as **pottery and porcelain**. Younger children could make rice bowls from thumb pots, which could then be painted and glazed; and the story of the Willow Pattern plate could lead to more sophisticated design work, using paper plates or clay.

The willow pattern story

Great was the power of the mandarins of old China, and great was their wealth. One such mandarin lived in a mansion two storeys high. While common men slept on the ground beneath humble roofs, the mandarin slept each night on a level with the blossom of his peach trees.

The gardens of his mansion were a paradise of pools and flowers, lawns, bridges and pavilions. But the greatest beauty in the gardens of the mandarin was the mandarin's daughter Li-chi.

The mandarin often worked all day in his library, with his secretary – a young and handsome man named Chang. While the mandarin ate sumptuous meals, Chang would walk in the gardens. He liked to stand on a bridge which led to the island of a large ornamental lake and watch the golden fish swim by below.

Li-chi too, loved to stand on the bridge and watch the golden fish. She loved still more to watch the sloe-black eyes of Chang and to drink in his words, as he spoke of Pekin and Anyang and the distant lands of Tibet.

Before long, Li-chi loved Chang, and Chang loved Li-chi – although he said, 'You are high above me, being the daughter of the mandarin. I am nothing but a humble secretary.'

'But you own a garden of wisdom and the flowers of poetry,' she said. 'You are therefore as noble and rich as my father. Let us stand beneath the orange blossom and promise to love one another for ever!' So hand in hand they stood beneath the orange tree and vowed vows of love. But the mandarin, sitting at his window upstairs, overhead them!

'Be gone, Chang! And never let me see your worthless, low-bred face in my garden, in my mansion or in my realm! How dare you talk of marrying her!'

So Chang was banished and Li-chi's tears fell, just as the willow began to shed its leaves into the glassy lake.

But under cover of night Chang crept back to the garden of the mandarin and called Li-chi's name in a whisper. 'Come away with me to my home which is farther than Anyang or Pekin and stands among the hills of Li.' She climbed down to him through the branches of the orange tree.

'We will hide in the gardener's hut on the island in the centre of the lake', said Li-chi. 'My father will never think of looking for me in so foul a place. Tomorrow night, when he has stopped searching, we will escape!'

So it was that they crossed their beloved bridge hand in hand, and hid all night in the gardener's hut, where earwigs crawled and spiders wove their webs, and silk worms glowed and wet slugs nestled.

All next day they heard the noise of the search. The mandarin's servants searched the mansion from top to bottom. They searched the pavilions and the flowery grove. They even shook the last leaves from the weeping willow, while the mandarin himself roamed his garden swearing vengeance on Chang.

Evening came. Huddled on their island in the gardener's hut, Li-chi and Chang kissed and prepared to make their escape.

But as they stepped on to the bridge to cross from island to shore, there, barring their way, stood the mandarin, a huge whip in his hand. 'There is no escape!' he shouted. 'I've trapped you, treacherous Chang. Prepare to die!'

Li-chi gave a cry of terror. 'Oh Chang, Chang, what have I done to you? There is no way off the island but across this bridge!'

On and on, the mandarin came, cracking his whip. It seemed certain that Chang would be beaten to death. 'Jump, Chang!' cried Li-chi. 'Jump with me into the water. For if we cannot be together in life, we shall be together in death!' And hand in hand they leaped to certain death in the waters below the bridge!

Great was the power of the mandarins of old China. But greater still was the power of the gods! Looking down from the mountain tops, the gods loved Li-chi and Chang for their faithfulness and courage.

Just as the mandarin's whip slashed the air where they had been standing, Li-chi's white arms were turned into the loveliest of feathers, and Chang's body dissolved into dove's down.

The gods had transformed the lovers into two turtle doves!

They flew far, far away – out of sight and out of reach of the cruel old mandarin. It is said that they built a nest, far away, among the hills of Li. And now all the world knows their story. For the potters of China painted it, in saddest blue, on finest porcelain, and sold their wares far across the seas – farther even than Pekin, Anyang, or the distant lands of Tibet.

Chinese food is familiar to many children and most towns have their own Chinese restaurants. Younger classes might set up their own restaurant at the time of the Chinese New Year, complete with publicity material, menus, and chopsticks obtained from a local source. Traditional food could be prepared and eaten, and the children might be issued with certificates to show their proficiency in using chopsticks.

Chapter 8

The Wind is Saying Spring

The earth stands mute, without a voice to sing,
But the wind is saying spring.

Helen Janet Miller

As the long, cold, dark days of winter draw to a close and evidence of regeneration can be seen all around, it is hardly surprising that many cultures celebrate this 'rebirth' with a special spring festival.

 One of the oldest spring festivals is the **Hindu** festival of **Holi**. Festivities, which can last for three days, begin with the collection of wood for a huge bonfire, that is lit on the Holi evening after a special service in the temple. The service includes symbolic use of the arti (a large plate holding divas – candles), which is passed among the worshippers, who warm their hands over the flames and then pass them over their foreheads. A prayer for forgiveness is read and followed by a reading in Sanskrit.

Lord, lead me from the wrong paths to the right,
From all wrongs to truth,
From darkness to light,
From death to immortal life.

All the worshippers put a coin on the tray as an offering. Then everyone receives the **prashad** (holy food of nuts and fruit) before going outside to gather around the bonfire. Coconuts are placed in the pyre before it is lit, and are later retrieved as prashad. The coconut is an important symbol in Hinduism. It is considered the perfect food, containing milk, protein and carbohydrate. Like a person, it is hard on the outside, but, once that person discovers the hidden truth about himself, he has found something perfect. The three eyes on the shell are said to represent the gods Shiva, Vishnu and Brahma.

Rubbish is burned on the fire, signifying the forgiveness of past misdeeds, together with an effigy of the legendary Holika. It is central to the Holi festival, and represents the triumph of good over evil by commemorating the victory of the young prince, Prahlada, over his wicked father, King Hiranya Kashipu.

St Cuthbert and the eagle

A number of saints' days are celebrated during the spring period, the most familiar being St Valentine's Day on 14 February, St David's Day on 1 March and St Patrick's Day on 17 March.

A less well-known legend with a simple moral related to caring and sharing, is the story of St Cuthbert, Bishop of Hexham in 684, and a man renowned for his love of the natural world. His special day is celebrated on 20 March.

One day Cuthbert was travelling over the hills of Scotland to a remote village, to talk to the people there about Jesus. He had with him a young boy called Cedda, who was showing him the way from Cuthbert's monastery at Melrose to the village. The boy had lived in the village all his life and knew the hills near his home very well, but the monastery was a long way from the village, and the boy was soon lost.

'I think it's this way,' he said, as they followed a rocky track in the biting cold wind. But a few miles further on the boy said, 'I think we're going the wrong way. I think we should be over there,' and he pointed in the opposite direction.

By now the boy was nearly in tears. He was shivering and hungry. He had no idea where they were and he knew that it would soon be dark. He was sure that Cuthbert must be angry with him.

'I'm sorry,' he said. 'I thought I knew which way it was.'

'Don't worry,' said Cuthbert. 'It's easy to lose your way in the hills. We'll go a bit further and then find a rock to shelter behind until morning. We'll be quite safe. God will take care of us.'

'But we've nothing to eat,' said the boy, starting to cry. 'And I'm so hungry. We might die of cold and hunger in the middle of the night.'

'God will take care of us,' said Cuthbert again. 'He cares for all his creatures. Look!' and he pointed to an eagle soaring high in the sky above them. 'The eagle doesn't worry about spending the night in the hills. God provides him with food and shelter, and God will take care of us, too.'

As Cuthbert and the boy watched, they saw the eagle hover in the air, its wings stretched out like fingers above them.

Then suddenly the eagle dived towards the surface of the river. It used its powerful wings to control it as it swooped low over the surface of the water. It extended its sharp talons and tipped its body backwards, then, with a splash of silver spray it lifted a huge fish, a salmon, out of the river.

The eagle tried to rise again into the air, but the fish was too big, too heavy, and it fell back to the rocks at the riverside. The eagle soared upwards and hovered, ready to try again to seize the fish.

'Quick!' said Cuthbert. 'Go and see if you can get the salmon.' But Cedda was already running across the grass and scrambling over the rocks to reach the fish.

He grabbed it before it could flip its way back into the water, and he held it high above his head, turning to grin at Cuthbert. 'Look!' he said excitedly. 'Now we can eat. I'll gather some wood. There's a dead tree over there. We can light a fire and cook the fish. There's plenty for both of us. We'll feel better when we've eaten.'

'Yes,' smiled Cuthbert. 'But you mean there's enough for all three of us! Look,' and he pointed to the sky, where the eagle still hovered, watching the man, the boy and the fish. 'He deserves his share of the food too,' said Cuthbert. 'After all, he caught the fish. God has provided enough food for all three of us.'

Cuthbert divided the fish into three portions. He took one part and put it back on the rocks at the edge of the river. Then he went to help Cedda gather wood for their fire. The eagle swooped to the rock and carried the fish off easily in its talons. Cedda and Cuthbert cooked and ate their portions of the fish.

As they were eating, Cedda suddenly pointed to a cluster of tiny lights, twinkling in a valley between the hills.

'There it is,' he said. 'There's the village we've been looking for.'

'God has indeed showed his care for us today,' said Cuthbert. ' He has provided food, and now he has shown us the way to shelter. He has answered our prayers.'

Jeanne L Jackson

Spring-cleaning

Spring-cleaning, or 'putting your house in order', is another symbolic gesture associated with this time of year. The activity is beautifully described in the opening chapter of Kenneth Grahame's classic story, *Wind in the Willows*.

The story of Persephone

One of the most enduring of the Greek myths is the story of Persephone – an appealing, allegorical explanation of the return of spring each year.

Once, long ago, when the world was young, Demeter, goddess of the Earth, lived with her daughter, Persephone, in the wonderful garden she had created. It was so full of flowers and fruits, so peaceful, that many of Persephone's friends and the animals and birds of the forest came to enjoy its quiet tranquillity.

News of the garden and the beautiful young girl who played there, reached the ears of Pluto, the god of the underworld, who vowed to take the maiden for his wife. One day, when Persephone was strolling alone, exploring the secret paths, smelling the fragrant flowers, watching the bees busy at their work, the evil Pluto snatched her and carried her off to Hades, his kingdom deep inside the earth. No one heard her desperate cries for help, and it was some time before Demeter discovered that her daughter was missing.

At first she thought Persephone was just hiding, playing a silly game, and she was very cross. But when her frantic shouts brought no reply she became more and more worried.

Anxiously she searched every corner of the garden, questioned Persephone's friends, but no one knew where her daughter had gone.

In desperation, Demeter asked Apollo, the sun god, if he had seen Persephone from his chariot as he made his daily journey across the sky. Sadly Apollo described how Pluto had seized the young girl and taken her to Hades to be his queen.

Demeter was overcome with grief. Too upset to care, she neglected the garden. The longer Persephone remained underground, the colder the earth grew. Its beautiful plants died and famine visited the land, bringing hunger and suffering. At last Zeus, god of the sky, looked down pityingly upon the barren earth and ordered Pluto to return the maiden, provided she had not partaken of the fruit of Hades. Full of hope, Demeter descended into the underworld, but bad news awaited. Persephone, pining for her mother, had resisted all food, save five seeds taken in a single bite from a pomegranate. On arriving at Pluto's court, Demeter was told of her daughter's deed, and returned distraught to the dying earth, fearful once more that Persephone would never be allowed to follow. Zeus, however, showed mercy, and wisely decreed that the young girl should spend part of the year, one month for each of the five pomegranate seeds eaten, with her husband in the underworld. During that time, the world would grow cold and the plants appear to die. Persephone's return in the spring, however, would herald seven months of warm sun when Demeter's garden would blossom and bear fruit once more.

Museum piece

Imagine not knowing about buttercups,
never seeing them light up the grass.
Imagine if one day you found one by chance,
how you'd keep it safe underneath glass.

Imagine missing the deep sea of yellow
if buttercups were incredibly rare.
You couldn't possibly hold one under
your chin to see a butter mark there!

You couldn't watch cows go paddling
in buttercups up to their knees.
You'd lock every flower up in a case
or preserve it in the deep-freeze.

Next time you find yellow buttercups
shining jewel-like under the sun,
look at a flower as though it were gold,
imagine it's the last precious one.

Imagine if nobody cares for the earth,
if buttercups die in front of your eyes –
that tiny frail flower you hold in your hand
might well be the world's greatest prize!

Moira Andrew

Growth often forms part of class topics at this time of year, and there are many stories which can be used to develop and expand the theme. In Claire Merril's book A seed is a promise, Scholastic Book Services 1973, she recounts the story of the prehistoric lemmings.

The prehistoric lemmings

One day, in the cold north country of Canada, a miner was digging in the frozen earth.

Deep down, he found some old animal burrows.

Inside the burrows were some animal bones.

Next to the bones were some tiny seeds.

The miner took the bones and seeds.

He showed them to some scientists.

The scientists found out that the bones were the bones of little animals called lemmings.

The bones were very old.

Thousands and thousands of years ago, in prehistoric times, the lemmings must have stored the seeds for food.

Everyone wondered, could such old seeds still grow?

Had the earth acted like the freezer in your fridge?

Had it kept the seeds from spoiling?

The scientists put the seeds on special wet paper and waited.

Two days later, they saw that some of the seeds had kept their promise.

They had sprouted after thousands and thousands of years.

In time, the seeds grew into healthy plants.

The plants grew flowers.

The flowers made new seeds – each with a promise of its own.

ADDITIONAL RESOURCES:

Welcome back Sun, Michael Emberley, Little, Brown and Co
The Dove, Dianne Stewart, Greenwillow Books
Fish is Fish, by Leo Lionni, Picture Puffin, explores several issues related to growth, including the nature of individual identity.

Treat the earth well

> *Treat the earth well*
> *It was not given to you by your parents*
> *It was loaned to you by your children.*

In spring, as the natural world wakens from winter dormancy, there are many opportunities to promote pupils' awareness of environmental issues, focusing initially upon the school building, its immediate environs and the local area, and then extending to address wider global problems.

Operation Springclean

This story features an organised 'litter-pick'.

We couldn't believe our luck. We'd only gone about twenty metres inside the spinney when we found a settee and two broken doors. Wayne was really impressed.

'That sofa's better than the one we've got at home,' he said 'If we could find the chairs we'd have a three-piece suite.'

We were building a den. The spinney's just along the street from my house and it's our favourite place to play in the school holidays. Better than the leisure centre, better than the park, because it's free and there are no notices saying 'Keep off the grass', or 'Don't climb the trees', and there's plenty of junk lying about to use for our dens. People just park along the road, open their car boots and dump their rubbish. Some even bring it in wheelbarrows and tip it amongst the brambles.

We dragged the doors and settee deeper into the undergrowth and searched for a good place to start the shelter. By the look of the sky we'd have to hurry. It was going to rain. The collection didn't take long to grow. We balanced wooden pallets on empty oildrums, laid broken pieces of plasterboard alongside and covered the lot with a sheet of polythene weighed down with bricks, a few plastic traffic cones, the odd supermarket trolley and a few old paint tins for good measure.

We finished just in time. The first spots were beginning to patter on the roof as Steve and me rolled about on the settee having friendly wrestling matches. But Wayne couldn't stop admiring the den.

'It's brilliant,' he said. 'The best ever. I could live in here.'

I didn't think I could, but I was proud of our work. It was a great den. Until someone started stealing it. Not that I heard anyone of course. I was too busy playing about, but Wayne did.

'Sh! Quiet! Pack it in!' he whispered. 'There's someone outside.'

We stopped fighting and listened. He was right. And they were messing about with the shelter.

'I'll count three,' he said, 'then we'll charge outside and get him.'

I wasn't so sure.

'What if it's an old lady with a dog. A Rottweiller?'

'We'll just say hello ... and sorry. Right? Okay! One ... Two ... Three.'

It wasn't an old lady. Or a Rottweiller. It was a drenched Lee Toms and he was walking off with one of our traffic cones in each hand.

'Tomsy!' we shouted. 'Come back!'

But he took no notice. He needed sorting out. Wayne and me snatched the cones and Steve grabbed Lee.

'What's your thieving game, Tomsy? This is our den.'

He didn't get a chance to answer. A bedraggled figure in an anorak appeared through the undergrowth.

'Well done, boys,' he said.

I knew that voice. Mr Coleman, our teacher. Was there no escape? We were supposed to be on holiday.

'Tremendous. You *have* been busy.'

First he inspected the great heap of rubbish around the den and then he looked at us.

'Wayne, Steven and Gary. I didn't even realise you were coming. Did you put your names down on my list? Well, never mind, you've done really well so far, brilliant!'

And then I remembered. His precious 'Operation Springclean'. He'd asked for volunteers to help clear up the spinney in the holidays, and today was the day. We'd certainly made a good start, even if we weren't supposed to be there at all.

'That way boys, the skip's over near the road.'

Bit by bit we dismantled the den and carried the pieces to the waiting container. The rain was heavier now and we were soaked through. Wayne grumbled the whole time.

'Best den we ever made,' he moaned, 'and it finishes up on a rubbish skip.' But I was beginning to enjoy it. When we'd shifted all the big stuff (the car batteries, rubber tyres, broken television sets, rusty bicycles) we started to collect litter in black plastic sacks. There was so much lying about, it didn't take long to fill one.

At last the spinney began to look like the woodland in one of those wildlife films. I wouldn't have been surprised to see a deer or a red squirrel or David Attenborough appear at any minute. By dinner time the skip was filled so high we couldn't reach to put any more sacks on top.

'Okay!' Mr Coleman shouted. 'Gather round everybody.'

He waited until we had all assembled around the skip before unzipping his sports bag and taking out a pile of papers.

'Well done, everyone. What a super job. Look at the difference you've made. Let's hope the litterbugs get the message. You've all earned your Operation Springclean certificates.'

Then he called us out, one at a time, and made the presentations. I slipped mine inside my coat to keep it dry and hurried home.

Mum was in the kitchen loading the washing machine. I showed her the certificate but she didn't seem as excited as Mr Coleman had been. In fact she nearly went spare.

'What on earth have you been doing, Gary? You're soaked! Look at the state of you. Get out of those filthy things and into the bath, NOW!'

There was no use arguing. I started to unpeel my saturated clothes but Mum wasn't finished yet.

'And when you've had your bath, Gary ... '

She held up the certificate.

'Operation Springclean 2. Tidy your bedroom, please. It's a disgrace!'

Ian Addis

Crab's kingdom

This allegorical story explores the effects of pollution on a small rock-pool.

In the beginning there was a rock pool.

It was older than human memory. Year after year the sea had worn away at the rocks until the pool was a smooth hollow. When the tide came in, the pool became shadowy and mysterious. When the tide went out it became a shining basin of clear water. It never overflowed and never became dry.

The pool was a kingdom of its own. If you looked into its depths you could see many living things: fish and starfish, silent limpets and lively hermit crabs, shrimps and sea anemones. And sometimes, if you watched carefully, you could see a creature with a fine shell of mottled brown and white.

That was Crab, the king of the rock pool.

Like most kings, Crab had a rather good life.

He had long legs and sharp pincers. He could run faster than any other creature in the pool. He was the strongest animal in his kingdom, and he could not help being rather proud.

He lived in a dark hole under a ledge of rock. Near his stronghold the pool was shallow and its floor was flat and sandy. But at the other end, where the water was deeper, a forest of feathery weeds grew right up to the gateway which led into the open sea.

Sometimes, when the weather was stormy, the tide would wash some strange creature into the pool, but usually life in the pool was peaceful. Tides rose and fell, bringing in food and fresh water. The sun shone by day. At night the pool gleamed under the dark sky.

At least, that was how things were until the day when the invasion began ...

It began like any other day. The first specks of sunlight touched the pool. The Crab went out of his stronghold and felt the swirl of water around him. The tide was coming in. It was time to go hunting.

The Crab set off towards the forest. On his way he greeted the quiet contented limpets and the hermit crabs which scuttled about in their funny top-heavy shells.

The Crab took a narrow path which led to the depths of the forest. The tall weeds waved close around him. The sunlight disappeared.

Suddenly the Crab stopped.

In the darkness ahead he could see something strange. It lay near the entrance to the pool. Perhaps it was some unknown enemy from the sea beyond? The Crab gathered his courage and sidled towards the stranger.

It was not like anything he had ever seen before. It was long and shining, almost like a fish, but it was not a fish. It didn't seem to be alive. It drifted on the surface of the pool. It gleamed coldly in the sunlight.

The Thing remained there all day. By the next morning it had sunk to the bottom of the pool. Little by little the creatures in the pool became used to the strange Thing. Soon the hermit crabs were playing around it without fear.

But before long, two more strange Things had appeared in the little kingdom. One was like the first invader. The other was quite different. It was soft and waving, like weed, but had no colour. It floated round the pool, and at last became stuck in a crack of rock, almost blocking the entrance to Crab's stronghold.

As time went on, more and more strange Things arrived. Some were large and some were small, some hard and some soft. They were all different shapes and colours. Not one of them was alive, but unlike dead things they did not fade and disappear.

The beautiful pool became dirty and crowded.

One day, the Crab climbed out of his pool to lie in the sun. He had just stretched himself out on a dry sandy rock when he noticed a strange sight. A line of hermit crabs was coming out of the pool. When they saw him, they tried to hide.

'Where are you going to?' asked the King Crab.

The hermit crabs shuffled about uncomfortably.

'Well, you see, Your Majesty,' said one of them, 'we've decided to leave the pool. It used to be a nice clean place, but ever since those strange Things started to appear, the water's been getting dirtier and dirtier. We can't live here any more. We're going to find another pool ...'

The King Crab was silent. There was nothing he could say. He looked down at his pool. Sure enough, its waters were becoming grey and dirty.

'Go,' he said softly. 'Go, and I wish you good luck. But I will stay in my pool. Good-bye.'

For a long time he stared down at his kingdom, spread out below the smooth, sunny rocks. When he looked round, the hermit crabs had gone. Slowly, Crab crept back into his pool.

The next morning, when Crab left his stronghold, he realised at once that something was seriously wrong.

The tide had stopped. The water was not flowing in from the sea. All was as still as death. Not a ripple stirred in the pool.

Then the Crab saw what had happened. A cluster of strange Things had become wedged among the rocks. They were completely blocking the narrow gateway which joined the pool to the sea beyond.

The Crab was horrified. The tide from the sea was the lifeblood of the pool. Without it, how could he find food? How could the water in the pool stay fresh? Already he could feel the murky stillness poisoning his body. He ran to the gateway and tore at the Things with his strong claws, but his grasp slipped on their slimy surface. The Things remained as firmly stuck as ever.

They have won, thought the Crab. They have killed my world. But I have only one kingdom. I cannot leave it. I will stay here until I die.

But if only, he sighed, if only someone could rescue my kingdom ...

That same morning a boy came to the seashore. He walked barefoot over the rocks.

Now and then he stopped to pick up twisted shells or smooth pebbles. Best of all, he liked to gaze into rock pools. At first he could see nothing in them but sea water and weeds. But then he saw that they were full of life. He saw the darting specks of fishes. He watched anemones slowly changing from blobs of jelly into delicate flowers. It was like discovering a new world.

But the boy found one pool which was not full of life. It was close to a beach which had become covered with rubbish.

Picnickers had left empty cans and bottles on the sand. The tide had washed up plastic bags and broken toys.

The waters of this pool were grey and dirty. Nothing seemed to move in them except for evil bubbles which rose to the surface with a plop.

It was Crab's kingdom.

The boy felt sad when he saw the pool. He decided to clean it.

First, with a sharp stick, he fished out all the rubbish which floated on the pool. He cleared its blocked entrance, and he collected all the other litter which was scattered over the rocks and sand.

Then the boy began to dig a pit in the sand. The sun grew hot overhead, but still the boy dug. By noon he had made a deep, dark hole in the beach. He pushed all the rubbish into the hole and covered it with a thick layer of sand.

Next he found some pieces of wood and made large signs. The signs read:

PLEASE DO NOT THROW YOUR RUBBISH HERE.

He put two signs on the beach and one on the rocks. Then he went home. Darkness gathered above the sea. The inky waves broke over the empty, clean sand and the shining rocks.

The boy went back every day to look at the pool. The tide had begun to flow again. The sea washed away the stagnant water and the dead weeds. But still there seemed to be no life in the pool.

Then on the third day the boy saw something moving. Slowly, a creature appeared from under a ledge of rock. It was a crab. It had a mottled brown and white shell. It moved slowly, as if it was dazed, but even so the boy could see that this was the king of the pool.

To the Crab, it seemed as if it had all been a dream.

The strange Things which had almost killed his kingdom went as they had come, into the unknown.

The tide flowed. Light shone through water. Plants grew again. Slowly, the other creatures returned: the fish, the starfish, the anemones, and last of all the hermit crabs, timidly scuttling back to their old home. In a small corner of the wide sea life began again, almost as if nothing had happened.

Tessa Suzuki-Morris

ADDITIONAL RESOURCES:

The Whales' Song, Dyan Sheldon and Gary Blythe, Hutchinson
The Giant, Juliet and Charles Snape, Walker Books
Dinosaurs and all that rubbish, Michael Foreman, Puffin Books
Dear Greenpeace, Simon James, Walker Books

The banyan tree

Conservation awareness has been greatly promoted in recent years and children are increasingly familiar with many of its key issues.

The Qur'an says,

> *Even looking after plants and trees is an act of virtue. For a Muslim, it is an act of charity to plant a tree or till a land where birds or men or animals come and eat of its fruits.*

The question of achieving a balance between man's needs and his responsibility for the natural world is a difficult one. The stories of the Banyan tree and the Chipko movement (page 121) can be used to provoke and stimulate discussion and debate, which could be extended to encompass such contentious issues as vivisection, animal rights, blood sports, conservation of tropical rainforests etc.

Far away in India, in the heart of a great forest, there stood a mighty banyan tree.

The huge tree was home to many different creatures – the mice that burrowed beneath its roots, the beetles that crawled under its bark, the bees that swarmed inside its trunk, the monkeys that swung in its branches, and the birds that nested amongst its leaves.

But to the woodcutter it was just a tree. As he stood beneath its giant canopy, shaded from the hot sun, he said,

'If I cut through the trunk with my sharp axe and bring the tree crashing to the ground it will make me a rich man. I can take the wood to market, make lots of money, buy a piece of land and build a house, find a wife and raise a family.'

The creatures in the tree listened to his words with alarm.

'The tree is our home,' squeaked the mice from their burrows beneath its roots. 'Please don't chop it down.'

'The tree is our home,' chirruped the beetles from their holes under its bark. 'Please don't chop it down.'

'The tree is our home,' hummed the bees from their honeycomb inside its trunk. 'Please don't chop it down.'

'The tree is our home,' squealed the monkeys from their hiding places amongst the branches. 'Please don't chop it down.'

'The tree is our home,' sang the birds from their nests amongst the leaves. 'Please don't chop it down.'

'This is where we live,' chorused all the creatures. 'PLEASE DON'T CHOP IT DOWN!'

But the woodcutter had a stony heart.

'I don't care about that,' he said. 'I want to cut the tree down and I shall. It will make me rich. So clear off all of you, before you get hurt.'

And he lifted the axe above his head as he prepared to strike the first blow.

But the creatures were angry. The beetles and bees stung his hands and flew into his face. The monkeys gathered on the branches and pelted him with fruit. The birds swooped down and pecked at his hair. Even the timid mice crept out to nibble at the laces of his great heavy boots. And they didn't stop until the frightened woodcutter threw down his axe and ran as far from the forest as his legs could carry him, never to return.

The mighty banyan tree still stands in the heart of the great forest and is home to many creatures. The mice beneath its roots, the beetles under its bark, the bees inside its trunk, the monkeys on its branches, and the birds nesting among its leaves.

Ian Addis

The Chipko movement

Some years ago, in northern India, there was a company which made sports goods. Some of the things they made needed a special kind of wood, and they heard about a forest hundreds of kilometres away where lots of these ash trees grew. The forest didn't belong to anyone, but the government said that only people who paid money for a licence were allowed to cut down the trees. The sports goods company decided it would be worth paying a lot of money to get that licence, so that only they could have the trees.

They hired a contractor and, one day in March 1973, some of the loggers arrived in the Gopeshwar forest to start felling ten of the trees. Much to their surprise, they were met by a group of local people who had come, not to welcome them, but to try to persuade them not to cut the trees down. The trees, said the villagers, belonged to everyone. For hundreds of years, the forest had provided the local people with shelter, firewood, food for themselves and their animals, medicines, and wood for their simple furniture and farming tools. Without the forest, they said, they couldn't live. The villagers also explained that the trees played a vital part in stopping the rivers from flooding in the rainy season, and helping to store water in times of drought.

But the loggers wouldn't listen to any of it. 'Our bosses have paid the government a lot of money to be allowed to cut down these trees,' they said. 'You haven't paid anything, so you can't stop us. You'd better go back to your village and let us get on with the job.' But then the loggers got their second big surprise. The villagers didn't go away – they walked quietly to the trees which had been marked, and threw their arms around them!

And there they stayed, hugging the trees, and daring the loggers to strike with their axes.

Of course, the loggers didn't want to injure the brave villagers, so they went back and told their bosses what had happened. It seemed for a while that the local people had won, but a few weeks later, they heard that the company were now going to chop down trees near another village, Rampur Phata, eighty kilometres away. At once, the people of Gopeshwar gathered together and set out to walk all the way to Rampur Phata. On the way, they sang and beat their drums, and all along their route people left their work and joined the march. When they arrived, they united with the local people and they all hugged the trees again.

This time the contractor's men didn't give up so easily. But the villagers were also determined, and the women in particular argued and protested for many months. Finally the contractor did give in, and to the great joy of all the local people, the loggers left.

That was not the end of the story. In fact, you could say it was the middle, because for many years before that, villagers in different parts of India had been struggling against their rulers and big business to save their trees. But these two particular incidents were the start of a huge popular movement which is still going on. It is called Chipko Andolan, which are the Hindu words for 'movement to hug'.

Everywhere local people, mostly women, are getting together to preserve their forests and their way of life. This is how one elderly woman described how she felt:

These trees are our heart.
These trees are our life.
One who will fell these trees will also cut us.
The one who will saw these trees will saw us instead of tree.
That's all.

Jill Brand

Leave them a flower

1. I speak on behalf of the next generation,
   My sons and my daughters, their children to come.
   What will you leave them for their recreation?
   An oil slick, a pylon, an industrial slum?

   Chorus

   Leave them a flower, some grass and a hedgerow,
   A hill and a valley, a view to the sea.
   These things are not yours to destroy as you want to,
   A gift given once for eternity.

2. You plunder, you pillage, you tear and you
      tunnel,
   Trees lying topppled, roots finger the sky.
   Building a land for machines and computers,
   In the name of progress the farms have to die.

3. Fish in an ocean polluted and poisoned,
   The sand on the beaches is stinking and black.
   You with your tankers, your banks and investments
   Say 'Never worry, the birds will come back.'

4. When the last flower has dropped its last petal,
   When the last concrete is finally laid,
   The moon will shine cold on a nightmarish
      landscape,
   Your gift to our children, the world which you've
      made.

Words and music by Wally Whyton

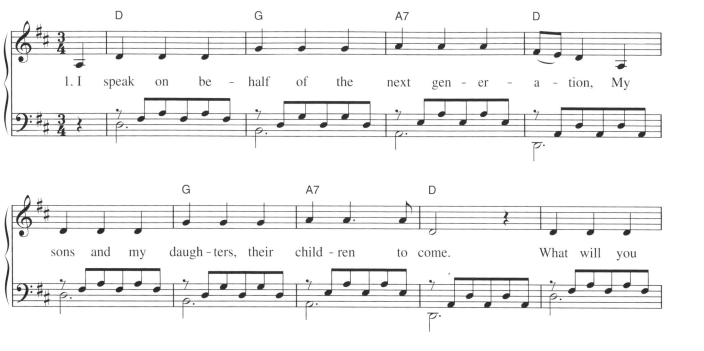

CHORUS

leave them for their re - cre - a - tion? An oil slick, a py - lon, an in-

-dus - tri - al slum? Leave them a flow - er, some grass and a

hedge - row, A hill and a val - ley, a view to the sea. These

things are not yours to des - troy as you want to, A

gift giv - en once for e - ter - ni - ty.

Poetry for Spring

First Primrose

I saw it in the lane
One morning going to school
After a soaking night of rain,
The year's first primrose,
Lying there familiar and cool
In its private place
Where little else grows
Beneath dripping hedgerows
Stalk still wet, face
Pale as Inca gold,
Spring glistening in every delicate fold.
I knelt down by the roadside there,
Caught the faint whiff of its shy scent
On the cold and public air,
Then got up and went
On my slow way,
Glad and grateful I'd seen
The first primrose that day,
Half yellow, half green.

Leonard Clark

Many thought-provoking poems on conservation can be found in *Earthways, Earthwise,* Nicholls, OUP.

Activities

Few topics lend themselves so readily to a range of cross-curricular activities as the theme of spring.

The natural world

Preparation for the spring 'awakening' may have taken place in the autumn with the planting of bulbs. A variety of seeds can be sown from late February for summer flowering/fruiting and their progress monitored. (Further details are given below in the section on planning a wildlife garden.)

One simple yet effective activity involves giving each child in the class a seed potato to plant – either in a suitable plot in their garden or the school grounds, or in a large container such as a bucket. Subsequent harvesting will produce a high yield at relatively low expense.

The school environment

Caring for and improving the environment in and around the school can provide a specific focus for pupils during this period of the year. Practical policies for dealing with the problem of litter on the school premises – posters encouraging tidiness, adequate bin provision, regular litter patrols on a class rota basis etc. – can evolve from pupil research into litter 'blackspots'. This can be extended beyond the school gates, especially if the school is in the proximity of a parade of shops. Findings may initiate correspondence with the local environmental health department.

The development of the school garden provides many children with opportunities to cultivate plants and develop a sense of responsibility and respect for plant life. Allocating areas for individual classes, year groups or Key Stages can accommodate a variety of approaches. Many schools have established ponds and wildlife gardens involving pupils at every stage in the process.

Establishing a pond and wildlife area

The benefits of establishing a pond and wildlife area in the school grounds are not restricted to curricular need but both help to improve immeasurably the immediate environment and provide children with a greater awareness and appreciation of wildlife habitats.

This section was contributed by JR Kemp, Science Co-ordinator, Barton Seagrave CP School who, with the involvement of pupils and the parent community, successfully introduced such an area in the grounds of a large urban primary school situated on a site with almost open public access.

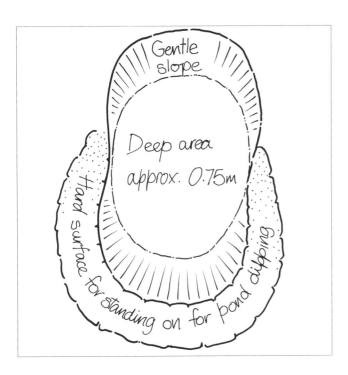

Creating a new pond

A pond needs plenty of sunlight to encourage plant growth. Avoid a site shaded by buildings or trees. It is almost certain that the pond will require topping up during dry spells in the summer, so ensure that there is a tap handy to which a hose can be connected. Ponds can be any size from an old sink upwards; the upper limits are obviously governed by the limitations of the site and your budget. In a small and perhaps enclosed area a glass fibre pond will probably be the best choice. For larger ponds, a butyl rubber will give the best service.

Having selected the site, the next job will be to mark out the edges of your pond. This can be done by using sticks, but a hose or rope is the best because the shape can easily be altered.

Excavation

Involve the children in the hard work of excavation in order that they develop a sense of ownership of the project.

Cut and remove any turf and stack this to one side. Dig out the hole and remove the soil to an appropriate spot. This can be planted with shrubs at a later date if necessary. Add another 15 cm or so to allow for protective layers plus soil at the bottom of the pond. Finally, cut a strip of turf about 50 cm wide all round the edge so you will be able to bury the edge of the liner. The size of the liner is determined by using this simple method:

Length of liner = overall length of pond plus twice the maximum depth.

Width of liner = overall width of pond plus twice the maximum depth.

Several weeks before beginning the project we asked parents for any old underlay or unwanted carpet. We put down a layer directly

onto the inside of the pond to protect the liner. The liner was placed into the hole and smoothed out, and another layer of carpet was placed on top. A 15 cm layer of poor subsoil or sand and gravel mixture was added, giving added protection and was used for planting into.

Fencing

It is important to consider the safety implications of a pond, and at this point it would be prudent to erect a substantial fence around the area.

Filling the pond

Put down a sheet of polythene, with line attached, and place the hose on top. This will lessen soil disturbance. Line the children up at an appropriate distance to watch, and turn on! When the pond is full, remove the polythene and trim off the liner and carpet, leaving an overlap of about 50 cm.

You will need an area of hard standing around part of the pond, where children can stand to pond dip. Use old slabs and crazy paving, ensuring that the lining goes under the edge.

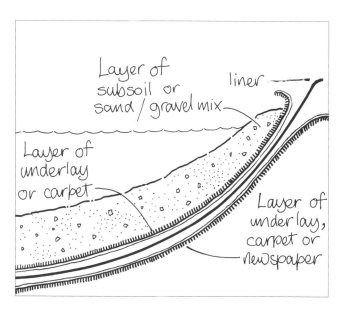

Stocking the pond

Allow two or three days for the dirty water to settle, and a few more days for the chemicals in the tap water to dissipate before planting, preferably in May. The plants will become established throughout the first spring and summer. Choose native plants because the animals that live in the pond are better adapted.

The following will form a sound basis, and give a good balance.

Submerged plants/oxygenators for deep water: Hornwort, Water Milfoil, Water Starwort

Rooted in deep water with leaves floating on the surface: White Waterlily, Water Crowfoot, Amphibious Bistort

Emergent plants for shallow water: Flowering Rush, Yellow Flag, Arrowhead, Water Plantain

Marsh plants for the edge: Marsh Marigold, Meadow Sweet, Water Mint, Brooklime, Water Forget-me-not, Sedges

Avoid Canadian Pondweed, Great Reedmace and Greater Spearwort as these can be invasive.

Pond animals

Insects will invade as soon as the first drop of water goes in. Diving beetles, water boatmen, dragonflies and damselflies will soon follow. Introduce water snails, frog and toad spawn (but not adults), the smooth or common newt and sticklebacks.

The wildlife garden

Mark out the approximate line of your hedgerow with sticks. Complete the perimeter using a football pitch line-marker and calculate the total length. This ensures the ordering of a precise number of hedging plants. To create a dense hedge use 75 per cent hawthorn and the rest a mixture of Field Maple, Guelder Rose, Hazel, Spindle Dog Rose, Wild Privet, Snowberry and Buckthorn. Later add Wild Clematis and Honeysuckle. Five hedging plants per metre should be your planting density. Plant any time during the winter up to the end of February, but not when the ground is frozen.

Children will enjoy helping with the planting.

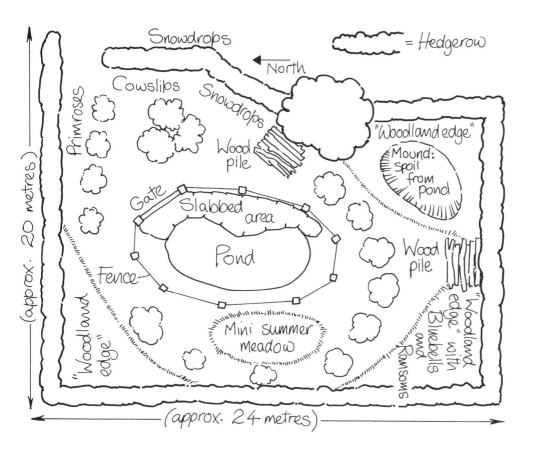

An 'edge of woodland' area can be created by introducing trees and shrubs such as silver Birch, Alder, Rowan, Crab Apple and Wild Cherry. Under the hedgerow and in the edge of woodland areas plant Snowdrops, Foxgloves, Bluebells, Red and White Campion and Ramsons (wild garlic). Children can sow the seeds in trays in the classroom – this gives them a feeling of participation and achievement.

The odd woodpile will provide shelter for insects and other invertebrates. Spiders will move in and after the minibeasts will come the birds. Birdboxes can be made in design technology lessons using the simple plan from the RSPB Young Ornithologists Guide (See address below).

A mini wild flower meadow can be developed by planting Ox-Eye Daisies, Knapweed, Yarrow, Musk Mallow and Meadow Buttercup.

ADDITIONAL RESOURCES:

The following will assist in preparing, planning and stocking the pond and wildlife garden.

Publications

How to Make a Wildlife Garden, Chris Baines
How to Make a Small Pond, Ursula Bowen, Berks, Bucks and Oxfordshire Naturalists Trust
School Nature Areas The British Trust for Conservation

Suppliers:

Water plants, pond liners, etc.:

Stapeley Water Gardens
London Road
Stapeley
Nantwich
Cheshire
CW5 7JL

Native wildflowers seeds and plants:

John Chambers Wildflower Seeds
15 College Street
Wellingborough
Northants
NN9 5PU

Suffolk Herbs
Sawyers Farm
Little Cornard
Sudbury
Suffolk
CO10 0NY

Native trees and shrubs:

Crowders Nursery
Lincoln Road
Horncastle
Lincolnshire
LN 9 5L7

Information on birdboxes etc.:

RSPB
The Lodge
Sandy
Bedfordshire
SG19 1MH

A wealth of information and advice on improving the school environment is available from Learning through Landscapes, 3rd Floor, Southside Offices, The Law Courts, Winchester, Hants SO23 9DL.

In the Bin	Household _____

What we throw away in a week

Paper/card	Metal	Waste food	Glass	Plastic

Re-cycling

Classes working on National Curriculum programmes of study relating to materials can investigate re-cycling by keeping a log of 'throw-away' items in common household use. School collecting points can be established, encouraging pupils to dispose of materials responsibly, e.g. drinks cans at lunchtime.

Energy saving

Promoting prudent use of energy resources can be encouraged by the design of posters for strategic use around the building and can be extended by awarding children 'Energy Saver' badges, in recognition of their awareness and practice.

ADDITIONAL RESOURCES:

Promoting Nature in Cities and Towns, Malcolm Emery, Croom Helm
Holding your Ground, Angela King and Sue Clifford, Wildwood House
A Guide to Habitat Creation, Chris Baines and Jane Smart, London Ecology Unit
Sharing Nature with Children, J B Cornell, Exley Publications
Developing Environmental Education in the Curriculum, Steve Goodall, David Fulton
Rescue Mission Planet Earth, Peace Child International, Kingfisher Books
Practical Conservation pack – Advice for Teachers, BTCV
The Green Umbrella, A & C Black

Chapter 9

The Secret Door

Books

*I know a secret door into
a thousand scary places
where there's bloodsucking vampires
and things that don't have faces.*

*A time machine that takes me
to fight with Francis Drake
and to fantastic jungles
on a magic silver snake.*

*I can leap into the future
on the Starship Enterprise
or crawl into a rabbit hole
and quickly change my size.*

I'm solving a murder mystery
you can follow me if you dare
while everyone around me
thinks I'm sitting on my chair.

I'm flying just like Superman
or riding painted wagons
I'm eating food in palaces
or killing fearsome dragons.

I meet Alice and Verucca
Gandalf and Captain Hook
I have a quite amazing time
when I sit and read a book.

Mike Hoy

In his introduction to the original National Curriculum English Orders, Professor Brian Cox wrote,

'Narrative has been described as a primary act of mind. Children construct the world through story. It is the teacher's role to recognise this and encourage it ...'

The importance of promoting literature, both to enhance reading standards and to offer a rich and varied source of stimulation and enjoyment, is well appreciated by schools. Good reading habits are constantly encouraged and reinforced through language programmes, access to well-stocked class and school libraries, and the occasional special events such as book fairs.

In recent years, many schools have introduced 'book weeks' (often coinciding with a national promotion during the autumn) when literature is given an even greater priority. As assembly frequently provides the focus for whole school participation and involvement, this chapter contains detailed background information, an extensive resource bank, and offers practical suggestions for follow-up or promotional activities supporting the theme.

Special books

The **Holy Bible** is the main book of the **Christian** religion and consists of the **Old Testament** and the **New Testament**. The Old Testament includes the story of the creation and is largely a history of the Jewish people. Its books were originally written on parchment in the Hebrew language, although some copies written in Greek still survive. It also contains extra books, called the Apocrypha, which form part of the Roman Catholic version of the Bible. The New Testament is a collection of stories and letters about Jesus and the beginnings of the Christian Church. It was written in the Greek language by some contemporaries of Jesus and other later converts to Christianity.

In 367 CE, Athanasias, Bishop of Alexandria, arranged the books and letters in the format which is familiar to us today. The four gospels (Matthew, Mark, Luke and John) contain accounts of Jesus' life, death and resurrection. The Acts of the Apostles, attributed to Luke, recount the experiences of the early Christians, while the letters (epistles), were written by prominent believers to members of newly-established churches over a wide area.

Various groups of Christians interpret the Bible in different ways. Some (fundamentalists) believe in its literal truth; some claim that, although the Bible is the 'Word of God', much of it is in the form of myths or allegories, each containing an important message; others emphasise the need for Christians to supplement their knowledge and understanding by reading the writings of believers from later periods of history.

Some of the most influential passages in the New Testament are the Parables. These stories, told by Jesus, address key spiritual and moral issues in an everyday context, many of which retain their relevance in modern society. Most familiar are 'The Sower' and 'The Tares' (Matthew chapter 13, Luke chapter 8), 'The Good Samaritan' (Luke chapter 10) and 'The Prodigal Son' (Matthew chapter 20). The 'Sermon on the Mount' (Matthew chapter 5) contains a comprehensive list of the qualities inherent in leading a Christian life, and in the following chapter (verses 9–13), the words from which the Lord's Prayer originates are recorded.

(Many excellent versions of Bible stories can be found in *Angels angels All Around* and *The Lion Storyteller Bible* by Bob Hartman, Lion 1995).

Attempts to contemporise the stories, however, often prove shallow and ineffectual, notable exceptions being *The Woodland Gospels*, Faber Fanfare, which offer a fresh, thought-provoking approach to the New Testament, and *Tales to Tell*, compiled by David Campbell, Holmes McDougall 1986, from which this version of 'Noah's Ark' is taken.

Noah's ark

The people in the village where this old carpenter lived were wicked – there's no other word for it.

They thieved and spoke foul language and told terrible lies about one another. They cheated each other right and left and they would sell their lovely daughters to the husband who offered most money. And they encouraged their sons to be even bigger twisters than themselves.

And the way they used animals was abominable! They hunted them down and worked them till they were nothing but hide and bone, then they took them to the knacker's yard and sold them for a pound or two. They would put out the eyes of songbirds to make them sing better.

133

'What's needed in this village,' said the old carpenter to his wife and sons, 'is a thorough *cleansing.*'

The carpenter and his sons began to carry planks of wood, saws, planes and boxes of nails, and hammers, up to the top of the ben. And there they laid the keel of a big boat.

How the villagers laughed when they saw that the old carpenter was building a boat up near the snow-line of the mountain.

'It's come at last,' they cried, falling over themselves with merriment and mockery. 'The old carpenter's gone off his head at last. He's bonkers! He's round the twist. We've seen it coming for a long time. How will the old fool get his boat launched from up there, near the sun?'

The whole village echoed with mockery for days on end.

The villagers laughed even louder when the old carpenter came down to the village post office and sent off telegrams to every species of animal and bird on earth, inviting them to sail with him and his family on the voyage.

They even drove up the mountain in their motor-cars to see how the ship was getting on. They had picnics up there. They pointed at the growing hull, and then fell about laughing. They took thousands of photos.

It was the greatest joke in years.

They took bets with each other as to how long it would be before the old shipwright was carted off to the mental asylum.

Then, from all the airts (directions) the animals began to arrive at the mountain, and climbed up to where the ship was having her final timbers set in place. And you couldn't see the new mast for the birds of every description that fell and furled on the rigging.

'Even the birds and the beasts have come to laugh at old Noah!' cried the villagers.

And at night the villagers would come and try to steal planks and pots of paint. But the snarling of the wild cats and the eagles' screams frightened them off, the scum that they were.

At first the villagers welcomed the rain, for it had been a hot dry summer. But when their thatches began to leak, and their cornfields were beaten flat, and the river began to rise, it was no joke. Night and day the rain fell, incessantly, for weeks on end. The river suddenly overflowed and the dam higher up burst its retaining wall, and the villagers, floating away as best they could on logs of wood and torn-off doors, saw the waters engulf the village and the farms. Those who left last saw that the ben (mountain) itself was awash half-way up. Presently the rising tide lapped at the boat with its cargo of innocents and birds and animals.

'Cast off!' cried Captain Noah from the bridge.

And the world was one huge ocean. And still the rain fell in tumults and torrents. And one after another all the scoundrels and twisters and liars that had infested the village for so long, drowned in the brimming sea of purification.

One morning, Noah the skipper let a dove fly from the ship, through the silver rain. Presently the dove returned with a branch in its beak. Then the sailors knew that the waters were receding, and the world was emerging new and green for good honest folk to live in.

Between the last raincloud and the golden sun lay a beautiful bridge of seven colours: the rainbow. Under it sailed the ship. And through the portholes the sailors could see the earth breaking like a butterfly from its chrysalis, pure and silent and lovely beyond words.

The **Jewish Bible**, or **Tenakh**, comprises the **Torah**, the **Nevi'im** and the **Ketuvim**. The Nevi'im contains the words of the prophets, the Ketuvim (writings), including the Psalms, but the Torah (teachings) is the most important. Its writings are of great significance for Jews, although diverse groups interpret its contents in different ways. Some regard it as a direct letter from God written down verbatim by Moses, some think that God gave Moses the ideas for the Torah which were then written down in human words, while others maintain that the teachings gradually evolved, incorporating new and different material over a lengthy period. But however Jews interpret the Torah, the same text is used by all.

The text includes stories about the children of Israel, and holy commandments containing laws governing worship and how to live, and it emphasises the special relationship existing between God and the Jewish people.

> *Be holy for I, the Lord your God, am holy.*
> *Love your neighbour as yourself.*
> *I am the Lord.*

The writings include the Talmud (oral teachings) and additional material resulting from early discussions about the Torah, the best known of which is Pirkei Avot (Sayings of the Fathers),

> *Who is wise?*
> *The one who learns from everyone.*

> *Who is strong?*
> *The one who controls himself.*

The reading of the Torah is central to Judaism, and over a year in the synagogue the whole book is read from beginning to end.

Muslims call the Qur'an 'Our Maker's Handbook'. They regard its contents to be the exact words revealed to the prophet Muhammad by the angel Jibriel, and, as such, they are Allah's final guidance for people everywhere. By the time of Muhammad's death, all the revelations had been recorded in the Qu'ran 'that which should be read'.

Many Muslims can recite the text by heart and all learn enough to perform their salah (daily prayers) in the correct way. The Qu'ran is divided into 30 separate sections, one for each day of the month, and into seven equal parts, for those wishing to read the whole book in a week. It is arranged into 114 'surahs', or short prayers, the most familiar of which is Al-Fatihah 'the opener', which Muslims repeat at least 17 times each day during the five occasions of salah. The final three lines express the special relationship between devotees and their God, Allah.

> *You alone we worship and You alone we ask for help.*
> *Guide us on the straight way, the way of those You have*
>   *favoured,*
> *Not the path of those who earn Your anger, nor of those*
>   *who go astray.'*

The **Guru Granth Sahib**, the holy book of the **Sikhs**, contains writings called Gurbani (the word of the Guru). It is written in the Punjabi language and all copies are exactly the same, each containing 1,430 pages.

The writings represent the teachings of the early Gurus, and those of Hindu or Muslim holy people, and were adopted as Holy Law by Guru Gobind Singh, the tenth and last Guru. Since then, the book has taken the place of the living Guru amongst Sikhs and is treated with appropriate reverence and respect. Every morning it is installed in the gurdwara with great ceremony, being placed on a platform beneath a canopy, resting on cushions. It is constantly attended by a worshipper who waves a fan over the book as a sign of its sovereignty.

On festive or special family occasions, the whole of the Guru Granth Sahib is read from beginning to end by a chain of readers. The reading is known as the **Arkhand Path** and usually takes about 48 hours to complete.

The book is written in poetic form, arranged in groups of lines called shabads. Its opening lines contain Guru Nanak's description of God (the Mool Mantra).

> *There is one and only one God*
> *Whose name is Truth.*
> *God the creator is without fear, without hate, immortal,*
> *Without form and is beyond birth and death*
> *And is understood through God's grace.*

Hindu scriptures (shastras) were passed down orally for centuries before being recorded. Written in the ancient Indian language of Sanskrit, the shastras are 'texts that explain and guide the way people behave in life'.

Most important among the texts are the Shruti (heard or created scriptures) which originate from the teachings of ancient wise men who are believed to have heard God's word directly. These include the four Vedas ('veda' means knowledge or wisdom) written some 3,500 years ago, and the Upanishads, a series of verses expressing the fundamental beliefs of Hinduism, recorded a thousand years later. The Upanishads contain ideas resulting from years of philosophical discussion between the older teachers (gurus) and their younger pupils, about the nature of the universe and why humans were created.

The Brihadaranyaka Upanishad

From the unreal
Lead me to the real

From the darkness
Lead me to light

From death
Lead me to immortality.

As many of the shruti texts were difficult for ordinary people to understand, the spiritual truths contained in the writings were often expressed through stories, and acted out in dance or dramatic form in villages throughout India. Most famous is the Mahabharata which tells of the adventures of the deity, Krishna, who visited earth in human form to teach people how to overcome evil and lead dutiful lives.

Buddhist teaching has been largely influenced by the doctrines of Theravada and Mahayana. The former, known as the Pali canon, contains the sermons, stories and Vinaya (rules of conduct) of Buddha, and was originally passed down orally by monks and nuns before being recorded in the Pali language of India some 400 years after the founder's death. Mahayana teaching utilises many different sources, some written in Sanskrit, others originating from Tibet, China and Japan.

One significant Buddhist teaching is the 'three signs of being'.

Life is always changing.
We suffer when we always expect life to be the way we like it.
We change also. What we call ourselves is not fixed, not a permanent self.

Another is about karma, which means 'action'. This maintains that people will always suffer the consequences of their actions, for good or bad.

The teachings urge Buddhists to seek the 'middle way' between extreme asceticism and worldliness. This is depicted as an eight-spoked wheel symbolising the Eightfold Path to Enlightenment which offers a way out of suffering.

Skills gained from reading

Before examining selected examples of the great variety of secular literature available, it may be pertinent to consider some of the cross-curricular skills to be derived from well-chosen, stimulating reading material.

In *Teaching children's literature in the primary school,* David Fulton 1990, Geoff Fenwick maintains that through story-telling and story-reading, children,
- '... develop listening skills;
- improve and increase vocabulary;
- increase reading competence;
- improve written and oral work;
- increase sensitivity;
- stimulate imagination;
- develop positive attitudes to books and reading;
- are introduced to a rich variety of literature;
- are encouraged to develop an interest in fantasy;
- come to terms with real-life situations;
- are made aware of their own and others' cultural heritage;
- are presented with a valuable shared experience.

From a wealth of possibilities, I have chosen a range of examples which are representative of their genre and which may prove helpful in attracting children, or teachers, to unfamiliar sources of material.

Myths, legends and folk-tales

Myths, legends and folk-tales from around the world provide a rich source of exciting, thought-provoking multicultural stories. Most are comparatively brief, quickly identify characters and conflict, and result in the triumph of good over evil. Their appeal extends across the primary age range, and we have a responsibility to preserve aspects of our literary heritage by familiarising children with the most important, including:
Classical legends, Norse legends, Tales of Robin Hood, the Arthurian legends, Aesop's fables, folk-tales from around the world, the Anansi stories, and the adventures of Brer Rabbit.

The story of the Minotaur

King Minos ruled the beautiful island of Crete. Beneath Knossos, his palace, there was a maze of dark passages called the Labyrinth. Here lived a terrible monster called the Minotaur. It had the body of a man, but the head of a bull – complete with large horns.

King Minos had defeated the people of Athens. He had made them promise to send seven boys and seven girls to Crete every nine years, to be fed to the Minotaur.

The sad time came round for the third group of young people to be sent to Crete. Then brave Theseus, the son of Aegeus, the King of Athens, stepped forward.

'Let me go too,' he asked his father. 'I may be able to find a way of getting into the Labyrinth and killing the Minotaur.'

'Impossible, son!' his father replied. 'And anyway, I couldn't bear to lose you.'

But Theseus would not take no for an answer. So, in the end, King Aegeus gave in.

'Oh, all right then,' he said, sadly. 'But I'll be watching out for your ship every day. Usually this ship comes back from Crete with a black sail. If you are successful, I want you to put up a white sail instead.

When Theseus got to Crete he met Ariadne, King Minos's daughter. She fell in love with him at once because he was so handsome. Theseus told Ariadne his plans.

'No one has ever been able to find their way out of the Labyrinth,' Ariadne said, 'It is so dark and there are so many twists and turns. But you can do it if you take this ball of thread and play it out behind you as you walk.'

In the dead of night Theseus went into the Labyrinth. As he walked deeper into those eerie, echoing passages, he played Ariadne's thread out behind him. On and on he went. Suddenly, there it was: he had come face to face with the terrible Minotaur!

When it saw Theseus with its blood-red eyes, the Minotaur let out a ferocious roar. Jets of fiery breath came screaming out of its nostrils. It lowered its huge horns and charged. And what a charge it was!

Theseus had no weapon with him, but he was a champion at boxing and wrestling. He lightly dodged the Minotaur's first charge. And the second. The third time the Minotaur charged, it crashed into the stone walls. *Bam!* Theseus seized his chance. He leapt on to the Minotaur's back, grabbed its horns and twisted its neck round hard. With dreadful gasps and groans, the Minotaur slowly sank to the floor. Finally it gave out a ghastly moan and died.

Using Ariadne's thread, Theseus was able to get out of the Labyrinth safely. Then Ariadne helped Theseus and the other boys and girls from Athens to find their way back to their ship.

Unfortunately, Theseus was so happy that he clean forgot to change the ship's sail. Aegeus, his father, was watching out for them as he had promised. When he saw the black sail, his heart broke – and he fell from the tall rock on which he was standing and was killed.

John Snelling

The chariot of the sun

This is a dramatised version suitable for whole-class presentation.

Narrator, Class group, Phaethon, Voices 1, 2, 3, 4 and 5, Helios, Child.

Narrator

Why does the sun shine? The Greeks believed that a god pulled the sun across the sky each day. We would like to tell you that story.

Helios was the god who drove the chariot of the sun.

Each day he would travel from east to west.

Class

Shining sun,
Where do you come from?
Where do you go?
Rising in the east,
Setting in the west.

(Helios travels from right to left holding model of sun-chariot.)

Narrator

At night-time he would return to his home and rest.
The next day Helios would make the same journey again.

(Helios walks slowly home. Moon can be seen.)

Class

Shining sun,
Where do you come from?
Where do you go?
Rising in the east,
Setting in the west.

Narrator

The moon appears.
Night-time again.
Helios is homeward bound.

(Helios returns home.)

Narrator

Thank you Helios.
That's why the sun shines.

Class

Or so the Greeks believed!

Narrator

Helios had a son.

Phaethon

My name is Phaethon.
I am the son of Helios.
My father no longer lives with us but I can see him each day.
There he goes ...

Class

Shining sun,
Where do you come from?
Where do you go?
Rising in the east,
Setting in the west.

Phaethon

That's my father.

Voice 1

No, he can't be your father!

Phaethon

It is my father!

Voice 2

Impossible!

Phaethon

Father!

Voice 3

We do not believe you!

Phaethon

Speak to me, Helios.

Voice 4

You are no better than us.

Phaethon

He did not look!

Voice 5

We do not need to pretend that our fathers are gods to make us seem important. We are happy to be what we are and you should be too!

Phaethon

I will prove that you are wrong!

Narrator

Phaethon decides to visit Helios.

Phaethon

Father!

Helios

My son!

Phaethon

A favour!

Helios

You have only to ask.

(He whispers in father's ear.)

Helios

Impossible!

Phaethon

Please!

Helios

No!

Phaethon

Please!

Helios

Never!

Phaethon

Please!

Helios

Oh, all right then.

Narrator

Phaethon had asked if he could drive the sun chariot across the sky.

His friends would see him and know that Helios was his father.

Helios

My horses are strong, you must keep to the proper path.
Do not go too high or too low.

Narrator

Up into the sky they flew.
All seemed to be going well.

Phaethon

My friends cannot see me.
I am too high.
I must take the horses lower so they know it is me.

Narrator

Lower they went.

Child

The tree tops were burnt.

Class

The tree tops were burnt
Cities set on fire
Cities set on fire
Crops destroyed.
Crops destroyed.
Rivers dried up.
Rivers dried up.

(Class make appropriate actions on repeated line.)

Voice 1

The horses were out of control.
They went higher.

Voice 2

The earth grew dark.

Class

The earth grew dark.
The seas froze over.
The seas froze over.
Crops did not grow
Crops did not grow.

People were very cold.
People were very cold.

Narrator
Phaethon cried out.

Phaethon
Please Father, help me!'

Narrator
But the sun god could do nothing.
It seemed that the whole world would die!

Narrator
And so it might have done, had not Zeus, watching as always from Mount Olympus, thrown one of his mighty thunderbolts and stopped the runaway chariot.

Everybody
Watch out! Here comes Zeus with the thunderbolt!
Helios found his chariot and slowly made his way home.
So that ...
He could begin his journey ...
All over again.

Class
Shining sun,
Where do you come from?
Where do you go?
Rising in the east,
Setting in the west.

Narrator
Thank you Helios.
That's why the sun shines

Class
Or so the Greeks believed!

(Adapted by Andrew Phillips)

Stories of religious devotion

The story of Caedmon

Caedmon lived in the north of England during the seventh century. He was a cowherd and, like the rest of the villagers, enjoyed the celebrations on feast-day evenings when everyone gathered to eat and drink and make merry.

It was the custom on such occasions for each person in turn to entertain the others with a song, accompanying himself on the harp. Caedmon was ashamed that he could not sing as well as his friends, and he would sneak away before his turn came to perform. One morning, however, when he woke up he remembered a song he seemed to have composed in his sleep. When his turn came to sing at the next village feast, instead of leaving, he stood up and sang his song and it was greeted with much enthusiasm and applause.

News of the beautiful song reached the Abbess of Whitby who summoned Caedmon to sing for her. She persuaded the simple peasant to become a monk so that he could best use his gift for verse. Caedmon later composed many other poems, mostly about subjects from the Bible, so that all men might learn about it more easily. He became famous, but his original song remains the one for which he is best remembered. It is the earliest datable English poem.

Now we must praise the guardian of the heavenly kingdom
The powers of the Creator and his thoughts,

The works of the Father of Glory as he, the Lord, appointed the
beginning of every wondrous thing;
He the holy Lord, the guardian of mankind, first created for the
children of men,
The heaven as a roof.

Then the Eternal Lord, Ruler Almighty, afterwards created all the
world,
The earth for men.'

The story of the Venerable Bede

In 679, Baeda, or Bede, entered the monastery at Monkwearmouth when he was just seven years old. The monastery had been established five years previously by Benedict Biscop (see chapter 12, page 180) on his return from Rome and was generously equipped with holy books. The young Bede divided his time between services and study, learning Latin and memorising psalms and hymns, working in the kitchen or on the monastery farm, and being taught how to inscribe and illuminate manuscripts.

Two years later, he moved to a new monastery at nearby Jarrow, where he was to spend the rest of his life. Shortly after surviving an outbreak of plague in 685, which swept through the monastery claiming everyone except the Abbot and himself, Bede welcomed Benedict Biscop back from his latest visit to Rome. He was laden with books, pictures and other treasures to enrich the two monasteries. The Jarrow library became the greatest in all England, providing Bede with a wonderful source of material for his studies. He was soon skilled in Latin, knew some Greek and was familiar with history and such science as existed at the time. Some of his early writings, completed during his twenties, were text books intended for the young boys in his care. From the age of thirty however, now himself a priest, he wrote books on more general religious subjects. The most famous are *On reckoning time* (*De Temporem Ratione*), which helped to establish the calendar, and '*The History of the Church of the English People*, which documents the period from Caesar's invasion of Britain in 55 BC to the year AD 731. For the latter achievement, Bede is often called 'The father of English history'.

In the spring of 735, despite failing health, he continued with the painstaking task of translating St John's gospel. According to a contemporary letter, Bede died on completing the last sentence, just as the monks in the church of the monastery were singing the first service of the Feast of the Ascension.

Ian Addis

Stories with PSE themes

Assembly is an ideal occasion to use story to address issues with PSE themes. Here is a list of books which can be used in this way.

All kinds of families
Not Now Bernard, David McKee
It's Your Turn, Roger, Susanna Gretz
Gorilla, Anthony Browne
The Julian stories
More Stories Julian Tells, Ann Cameron
Journey to the Volcano, Rose Tremain
The Finding, Nina Bawden
The Granny Project, Anne Fine
The Shrinking of Treehorn, Florence Parry Heide

Friends and relations
The Elmer stories, David McKee
We Are Best Friends, Aliki
Garth Pig and the Ice Cream Lady, Mary Rayner
Willy the Wimp, Anthony Browne
I Am David, Anne Holm
The Indian in the Cupboard, Lynne Reid Banks
The Present Takers, Aidan Chambers
Murdo and the Weather Child, Joyce Dunbar
The Battle of Bubble and Squeak, Philippa Pearce
I'm Trying to Tell You / A Bit of Give and Take, Bernard Ashley

Somewhere to live
Moving Molly, Shirley Hughes
House by Mouse, George Mendoza
The Cupboard Under the Stairs, Martin Waddell
The Dolls' House, Rumer Godden
Babylon, Jill Paton Walsh
Somewhere to Play, Karusa
The Village by the Sea, Anita Desai

Poetry

The following volumes are very useful for choral speaking:
The midnight party, Richard Brown, Cambridge University Press
Whisked Away, Richard Brown, Cambridge University Press
He said, she said, they said: poetry in conversation, edited Anne Harvey, Puffin

Activities

Book week

Preparatory activities can be begun weeks in advance by the **compilation of anthologies** based on class reading records. Children can then recommend titles they enjoyed to other pupils. **Competitions** promoting the event stimulate interest, and could include the design of posters, bookmarks, cover illustrations, ex-libris, or 'Who said that?' quizzes based on quotations. One simple ploy to encourage children to use the school library is to hide **'bookworms'** in selected copies. These can be exchanged for a gift from the book fair after correct answers are given to a range of questions about the book. Offering **book stamps** to be redeemed at the book fair, as a reward for reading progress, general academic achievement or exemplary behaviour, is a simple but effective method of promoting a positive school ethos.

During the book week itself, there are many ways of stimulating interest. Younger children enjoy the opportunity to dress as a character from a well-known book. **Role-play** can be taken further by transforming a convenient area of the school into Spot's kennel or Peter Rabbit's burrow for example, enlisting the services of an older pupil, classroom assistant or supportive parent to play the part, and inviting the children to visit with a list of questions about the stories.

Another effective activity is to ask groups of children to produce two-minute **'trailer tapes'** of extracts from a book, including a prepared reading, introductory and background music and sound effects. Adverts, posters, reviews etc. can be linked to the same title.

Timetabled **story reading sessions**, led by members of the school staff, governors, visitors (e.g. staff from feeder schools or local secondary schools), each reading their favourite stories, are an effective method of promoting literature, extending cross-phase liaison and developing community links.

Visitors could also include people from the **book trade – booksellers, publishers, printers, librarians**, etc.

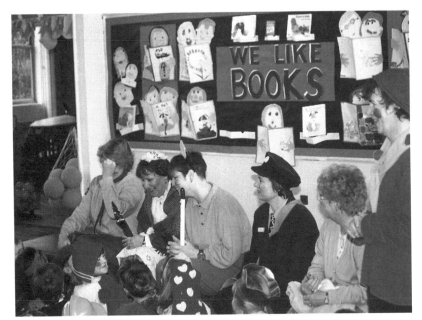

Many schools use the event as an opportunity to invite **established writers or illustrators** to talk to the children about their work. This might involve large group seminars where authors read extracts from their books or workshop sessions providing classes with practical advice on crafting stories or the skills of illustration. Local arts funding can sometimes be obtained to help with costs.

ADDITIONAL RESOURCES:

Meet the Authors and Illustrators by Stephanie Nettell, Scholastic Publications which contains 60 double-page biographies. *Looking for an Author?* is a directory of authors, illustrators and poets who participate in book events, obtainable from the Reading and Language Information Centre, Bulmerche Court, Earley, Reading RG6 1HY.

Many authors will correspond with children who write to them about their books. The exercise is useful both in encouraging familiarity with the stories and providing a practical exercise in letter writing. However it is advisable to keep questions brief.

There is considerable value for both parties in older children writing stories for their younger counterparts. The re-working of traditional fairy stories is a most effective and enjoyable activity, and the following titles provide examples of stimulating source material.

A Bad Week for the Three Bears, Tony Bradman and Jenny Williams, Picture Lions
Jim and the Beanstalk, Raymond Briggs, Picture Puffin
All the King's Horses, Michael Foreman, Hamish Hamilton
The Practical Princess and other Liberating Fairy Tales, Jay Williams, Hippo
Clever Polly and the Stupid Wolf, Catherine Storr, Puffin
The Three Little Wolves and the Big Bad Pig, Eugene Trivizas, Heinemann
Snow White in New York, Fiona French, OUP
Cinderella and the Hot Air Balloon, Ann Jungman, Frances Lincoln.

Chapter 10

The Turning of The Year

Easter

The year turns at Easter time
Button buds collect on the branches
and like a sprinkling of young yellow suns,
bright daffodils colour
the hibernating fields and hedgerows.
The year turns, slowly and silently, into spring
and everywhere the new born chicks, lambs and fledglings
struggle to be seen, heard and noticed.
Out of the grey, bare days of the weak winter
the sacred strength of spring emerges.
The year turns and Mother Earth lifts her ashen face
to the pale blue of the brightening sky.
In celebration she pushes up
the timeclocks of the ages –
a flourish of flowers, a blast of blossom.

John Rice

In many schools, the spring-time re-generation of life is closely linked to the Christian festival of Easter, the term culminating in a service or concert. This chapter focuses first on events in the Christian calendar leading up to Easter Sunday, the celebrations associated with those events and their implications for cross-curricular activities in school. It then embraces other spring festivals, notably the Jewish celebration of Pesach (Passover), the Muslim observance of Ramadan and the ensuing festival of Id-Ul-Fitr.

Shrove Tuesday marks the beginning of the Easter period. It was traditionally the occasion when Christians prepared for the lengthy period of abstinence due to begin the following morning, by eating, drinking and making merry. Fats, forbidden for the next 40 days, were mixed with eggs and milk and made into pancakes, resulting in the modern term 'Pancake Day'.

Shrove Tuesday is celebrated throughout the Christian world and in most French, Spanish and Portuguese-speaking countries is known as Mardi Gras or 'Fat Tuesday'. The day begins with the ringing of the Shriving Bell, calling people to church to be 'shriven' (absolved of their sins). At sunset, the bell signals an end to festivities and the beginning of the period of penance and fasting, known as Lent. Lent means, literally, 'the time of year when the days are lengthening' and corresponds to the 40 days and 40 nights spent by Jesus in the wilderness (Matthew 4:1–11).

In *Here's the Year*, (Julia McRae 1981), Peter Watkins and Erica Hughes identify the special significance of the number 40 in the ancient world.

'The 40-day span occurs again and again in the Christian Year and in religious literature: the 40 days from Christmas to Candlemas; the 40 days Jesus spent in the wilderness; the 40 days of Lent; the 40 days between Easter day and Ascension day ... The Bible is full of references to 40. It rained on Noah's Ark for 40 days. Moses spent 40 days on the mountain, and his life was divided into three 40-year phases. The Israelites wandered in the desert for 40 years. David reigned for 40 years ...'

On the first day of Lent, **Ash Wednesday**, many Christians attend a special service at which their foreheads are marked with a sign of the cross made from paste derived from the ashes of palm crosses kept from the previous year's Palm Sunday.

The fourth Sunday in Lent is known as **Mothering Sunday**. The festival has its roots in the Roman feast of Matronalia, and may also have been an attempt by the early Christians to suppress the pagan feast for Cybele, mother of the gods, which was celebrated in the spring.

People were required to attend the 'Mother Church' of the district, and this tradition probably led to 'absentee' sons and daughters going 'a-mothering', and returning to the family home for the day. During the eighteenth and nineteenth centuries, domestic servants were given the day off to visit their mothers, and often took a simnel cake (a fruit cake covered in marzipan) and bunches of spring flowers picked on the way. The day was also known as Refreshment Sunday, providing brief welcome relief from the Lenten fast. Mothering Sunday is often confused with Mothers' Day, now a somewhat commercialised parody of the initial concept which originated in the United States to honour all mothers regardless of colour or creed.

The last Sunday in Lent is called **Palm Sunday**. On this, the first day of Holy Week, Christians remember the story of Jesus riding in triumph into Jerusalem on a donkey, the streets lined with crowds shouting 'Hosanna' and waving branches of palm (Matthew 21:1–11).

The Thursday of Holy Week, **Maundy Thursday**, recalls the final meal shared by Jesus and his disciples before His arrest, trial and crucifixion (Matthew 26:20–30, John chapter 13). Elements of this 'Last Supper' are regularly re-enacted during the celebration of Holy Communion with the breaking of bread (the body of Christ) and the drinking of wine (the blood of Christ).

The story of the Last Supper

In 1495, Leonardo da Vinci began work on his famous painting depicting the event. Unfortunately, he used bright, strong, rich colours in tempera (ground colour mixed with egg yolk on dry plaster) instead of the usual fresco technique (water colour on fresh plaster), and the painting started to fall to pieces within 20 years. The modern picture is, therefore, a pale, shadowy, much restored version of the original. Da Vinci's choice of subjects for the painting has provoked much speculation over the years, and the following account offers an interesting explanation for his model for Judas.

Leonardo da Vinci was a genius. The colours he mixed and applied to canvas and plaster amazed the world. He was a gifted artist.

In 1493 the monks of Santa Maria delle Grazie asked Leonardo da Vinci to paint a mural in their monastery church. The subject of the painting was to be the Last Supper, showing Jesus sharing his last meal with his disciples. Leonardo decided to capture the very moment when Jesus was explaining to the disciples that one of them would betray him.

His research began. He planned to paint Jesus first; he needed someone who looked like his idea of Jesus. He found a young man who was ideal and agreed to be painted. Leonardo sketched, mixed and applied paint, gazing at the kind, caring face with sensitive features. He placed Jesus in the centre of the mural behind a long table in front of three windows.

After weeks of painting, Leonardo paid the young man several gold coins. The picture of Jesus was finished. Now he had to search for others whose features reminded him of each one of the twelve disciples. The months passed as Leonardo searched and painted – James, John, Simon Peter and Andrew the four fishermen, James, Philip and Matthew (the one rich man amongst the disciples), Thomas, a carpenter, Simon, Bartholomew and Thaddeus. He experimented with new techniques, paints and varnishes as he sought to make his canvas come to life.

After four years the mural was finished except for the face of Judas Iscariot, the disciple who betrayed Jesus.

Leonardo studied the faces of criminals, murderers and vagrants but none looked like his idea of Judas. In desperation he toured the narrow streets of the city of Milan, late into the night, staring into doorways and peering into the unwashed faces of homeless thieves and drunkards. Would he ever find the man he was searching for? One evening, a ragged figure leapt out of the darkness and hurtled threateningly towards him.

The sight of the villain's face shocked Leonardo. Never had he seen such a menacing expression with eyes brimmed full of hatred. He had found his Judas Iscariot.

When the man had calmed down, Leonardo asked to paint him. The stranger agreed immediately.

The mural of the Last Supper could now be completed. Leonardo positioned the final disciple, prepared his paints and sketching sticks and paused to study the bone structure of the rough and haggard profile. He stared intently, noticing that the lined, miserable face was drenched with tears.

The wretched fellow turned to face him. 'I was your idea of Jesus when you began this wonderful mural. Now, after four years of selfishness and greed, I am your idea of Judas Iscariot.'

Leonardo blended black into the startling white on his palette and began to outline the head of Judas with a threatening grey.

Sue Spooner

Jesus demonstrated his love for the disciples by washing their feet, a humble task usually reserved for slaves. It was a custom of the early Church for priests to follow Christ's example of humility by publicly washing the feet of twelve poor men of the parish each **Maundy Thursday**. Today, the Queen continues the tradition formerly adopted by medieval monarchs, albeit in a revised form, by handing out specially minted Maundy coins, one for each year of the sovereign's age, to selected elderly people. Attendant priests carry towels over their shoulders, a reminder of the original purpose of the ceremony.

Good Friday, the day on which Jesus was crucified, is the most solemn day of the Christian year. Bells remain silent, altars bare and priests wear black robes. Church services take place all day, but chiefly between noon and 3 p.m., traditionally the time of Christ's crucifixion and death (Matthew chapter 27, Luke chapter 23, Mark chapter 15, John chapter 19).

The custom of eating **hot cross buns** has existed for some 300 years.

However, cakes with crosses on were baked long before Jesus was born. Both the ancient Greeks and Romans ate similarly marked wheaten cakes in honour of Artemis, or Diana, goddess of the moon, the sections supposedly representing the moon's four quarters. Anglo-Saxons regarded the cross as a symbol of the pagan festival Eostre, held at the vernal equinox to venerate the goddess of dawn. It was the Saxon Christians, led by Saint Bede, who utilised many of the ancient names and symbols for their own spring festival – Easter.

In by-gone years, hot cross buns were supposed to have 'magical' powers', and were ground down to provide a powdered cure for sea-sickness. They were used by sailors as talismen to guard against shipwreck.

The **simnel cake** is also eaten at Easter-tide. Eleven almond egg shapes are put on the top, representing the Apostles. Judas, the disciple who betrayed Jesus, is omitted. (See *Marzipanned* in *Assemblies*, Scholastic Publications 1994.)

On **Easter Sunday**, Christians celebrate the risen Christ. Bells are rung, churches decorated with flowers, and black altar hangings changed to white. Some services begin at midnight with the church in darkness. A single candle, lit from a spark to represent the resurrection of Christ, initiates the illumination of the whole building. This candle, known as the Paschal candle, burns for 40 days, from Easter to the Feast of Ascension, symbolising the 'new light and understanding spread by Jesus'.

Like Pesach, Divali, Ramadan and the Chinese New Year, the date of Easter can vary from year to year. It is fixed as the first Sunday after the first full moon to occur after the vernal equinox (21 March). It must, therefore, fall between 21 March and 25 April.

There are numerous customs associated with the celebration, many of which involve eggs, which are symbols of rebirth and continuing life. Pictures survive of spring festivals in China, India, Greece and Egypt where eggs are used to depict fertility, and early Christians took eggs to church for blessing, as holy symbols of Christ's resurrection.

The practice of decorating eggs is long-established and widespread. The ancient Chinese exchanged red eggs at their spring festival. Centuries later, Polish villagers decorated eggs with Christian symbols such as the fish or the cross. In Hungary, flower patterns were used and in Yugoslavia, the letters X V, meaning 'Christos vakrese' or 'Christ is risen'. In Tsarist Russia, the court jeweller, Fabergé, fashioned beautiful jewelled eggs, while the less wealthy painted wooden replicas. Elsewhere, decorated and lacquered eggs of papier-mâché were made.

The modern chocolate egg originates from its sugar and marzipan forerunner, introduced some 100 years ago. The enduring appeal of the Easter bonnet probably reflects the old custom of renewing the wardrobe, and marking the change of season with a new set of clothes.

Join with us, Book 2, by Jeanne L Jackson (Stanley Thorne 1992) contains *The Legend of The Bells*, which features the traditional eggs, and also *The Legend of the Easter Rabbit*. The hare was once the sacred animal of Eostre, the pagan spring goddess, but has now been supplanted by the rabbit as a popular symbol on Easter greeting cards.

The Selfish Giant

Oscar Wilde's 'The Selfish Giant' can be adapted for dramatisation.

Every afternoon, as they were coming from school, the children used to go and play in the giant's garden. It was a large lovely garden, with soft green grass. Here and there over the grass stood beautiful flowers like stars, and there were twelve peach trees that in the spring-time broke out into delicate blossoms of pink and pearl, and in the autumn bore rich fruit. The birds sat on the trees and sang so sweetly that the children used to stop their games in order to listen to them. 'How happy we are here!' they cried to each other.

One day the giant came back. When he arrived he saw the children playing in the garden. 'What are you doing there?' he cried in a very gruff voice, and the children ran away. 'My own garden is my own garden,' said the giant. 'Anyone can understand that, and I will allow nobody to play in it but myself.' So he built a high wall all around it, and put up a notice board.

TRESPASSERS WILL BE PROSECUTED

He was a very selfish giant.

The poor children now had nowhere to play. They tried to play on the road, but the road was very dusty and full of hard stones and they did not like it. They used to wander round the high wall when their lessons were over, and talk about the beautiful garden inside. 'How happy we were there,' they said to each other.

Then the Spring came, and all over the country there were little blossoms and little birds. Only in the garden of the selfish giant it was still winter. The birds did not care to sing in it as there were no children, and the trees forgot to blossom. Once, a beautiful flower put its head out from the grass, but when it saw the notice board it was so sorry for the children that it slipped back into the ground again, and went off to sleep. The only people who were pleased were the Snow and the Frost. 'Spring has forgotten this garden,' they cried, 'so we will live here all the year round.' The Snow covered up the grass with her great white cloak, and the Frost painted all the trees silver.

'I cannot understand why the Spring is so late in coming,' said the selfish giant, as he sat at the window and looked out at his cold white garden, 'I hope there will be a change in the weather.' But the Spring never came, nor the Summer. The Autumn gave golden fruit to every garden, but to the giant's garden she gave none. 'He is too selfish,' she said. So it was always Winter there.

One morning, the giant was lying awake in bed when he heard some lovely music. It sounded so sweet to his ears that he thought it must be the King's musicians passing by. It was really only a little linnet singing outside his window, but it was so long since he had heard a bird sing in his garden that it seemed to him to be the most beautiful music in the world. 'I believe the Spring has come at last,' said the giant, and he jumped out of bed and looked out.

What did he see?

He saw a most wonderful sight. Through a little hole in the wall the children had crept in, and they were sitting in the branches of the trees. In every tree that he could see there was a little child. And the trees were so glad to have the children back again that they had covered themselves with blossoms and were moving their arms gently above the children's heads.

It was a lovely scene, only it was still Winter. It was the farthest corner of the garden, and in it was standing a little boy. He was so small that he could not reach up to the branches of the tree, and he was wandering all around it, crying bitterly. The poor tree was still quite covered with frost and snow, and the North Wind was blowing and roaring about it. 'Climb up, little boy,' said the tree, and it bent its branches down as low as it could, but the boy was too tiny. And the giant's heart melted as he looked out. 'How selfish I have been,' he said, 'now I know why the Spring would not come here. I will put that poor little boy on the top of the tree, and then I will knock down the wall, and my garden shall be the children's playground for ever and ever.' He was really very sorry for what he had done. So he crept downstairs and opened the front door quite softly, and went out into the garden.

But when the children saw him they were so frightened that they all ran away, and the garden became Winter again. Only the little boy did not run, for his eyes were so full of tears that he did not see the giant coming. And the giant stole up behind him and took him gently in his hand, and put him up into the tree. And the tree broke at once into blossom, and the birds came and sang on it and the little boy stretched out his two arms and flung them round the giant's neck and kissed him. And the other children, when they saw that the giant was not wicked any longer, came running back, and with them came the Spring. 'It is your garden now, little children,' said the giant, and he took a great axe and knocked down the wall.

When the people were going to market at twelve o'clock they found the giant playing with the children in the most beautiful garden they had ever seen. All day long they played, and in the evening they came to the giant to bid him goodbye. 'But where is your little companion?' he said, 'the boy I put into the tree?'

The giant loved him the best because he had kissed him. 'We don't know,' answered the children, 'he has gone away.'

'You must tell him to be sure and come here tomorrow,' said the giant. But the children said that they did not know where he lived, and had never seen him before; and the giant felt very sad.

Every afternoon, when school was over, the children came and played with the giant. But the little boy whom the giant loved was never seen again.

Years went over, and the giant grew very old and feeble. He could not play about any more, so he sat in a huge armchair, and watched the children at their games, and admired his garden. 'I have many beautiful flowers,' he said, 'but the children are the most beautiful flowers of all.'

One Winter morning, he looked out of his window as he was dressing. He did not hate Winter now, for he knew that it was merely the Spring asleep, and that the flowers were resting. Suddenly he rubbed his eyes in wonder, and looked and looked. It certainly was a marvellous sight. In the farthest corner of the garden was a tree quite covered with lovely white blossoms. Its branches were all golden, and silver fruit hung down from them, and underneath it stood the little boy he had loved.

Downstairs ran the Giant in great joy and out into the garden. He hastened across the grass and came near to the child, and when he came quite close his face grew red with anger and he said, 'Who has dared to wound thee?', for on the palms of the child's hands were the prints of two nails, and the prints of two nails were on the little feet.

'Who has dared to wound thee?' cried the Giant, 'Tell me, that I may take my big sword and slay him!'

'Nay,' answered the child, 'but these are the wounds of love.'

'Who art thou?' said the Giant, and a strange awe fell on him and he knelt before the little child. And the child smiled on the Giant and said to him 'You let me play in your garden. Today you shall come with me to my garden, which is Paradise.'

And when the children ran in that afternoon they found the Giant lying dead under the tree, all covered with white blossoms.

The Easter tree

This story by Richard Pinner can be adapted for dramatisation.

Readers 1, 2, 3, 4, 5 and 6, 1st Voice, 2nd Voice, Mallorn, Smee, and Frith.

Reader 1   To begin with, there was nothing. Then, slowly, there appeared two points of light, like cats' eyes in the dark.

Reader 2   One was golden, called the sun: and the other was silver, called the moon. And they shone on the world.

Reader 3   Then, deep in the earth, beneath a valley, there was a movement. A seed which grew into a tree, straight and noble.

Reader 4   And, beside the tree, a tiny spring bubbled into a nearby hollow – to make a pool of clear, shimmering water. And, beside the water, there grew a sprinkling of cornstalks, green at first but turning gold in the sunlight.

Reader 5   And so the seasons went by – Autumn, Winter, Spring, Summer. While the tree, with its evergreen branches bowing to the ground, became a place to shelter for the passing birds and animals, keeping out the howling winds of Winter and the scorching heat of the Summer ... until, one day, three people stumbled upon the place

Reader 6   Mallorn and her two sons, Smee and Frith.

                   This place was so peaceful – the boys so happy. Perhaps they could stay there, near the tree ... Then, slowly, Mallorn began to forget her worries and drift off to sleep – and, as she slept, she dreamt that there was a voice in the heart of the tree calling her ...

1st Voice   Mallorn ... Mallorn ... Mallorn ... if you listen to my words, you will never be without food and drink – even in the long winter months ...

Mallorn   Never?

1st Voice   Never! At least, not if you listen to me carefully ... When you awake, with the help of your sons you may cut the corn. But do not be greedy ... Half of the ears of corn you must sow back in the earth for next year – and the other half you must store, taking only a little each day to last you through the year ...

Mallorn   Sow half and store half.

1st Voice   In this way, you will survive right through the Winter – and in the Spring I will speak to you again ...

Reader 1   So Mallorn awoke – and followed the instructions of the Voice, to the letter. She sowed half and she stored half: and, sure enough, they all survived through the Winter as the Voice had promised. And, with each passing year, Mallorn had the same dream.

Reader 2   But as the corn grew taller, so did Smee and Frith: and year by year they demanded more and more corn ... until one cold Winter night, when Mallorn and Frith were out looking for twigs for the fire, Smee was left huddled in the snow. And, suddenly, he heard another voice ...

2nd Voice   Smee ... Smee ... Smee ...?

Smee   Yes ... who are you? What do you want?

2nd Voice   You're hungry aren't you? ... I know it's none of my business, but it does seem silly when you've got a great store of food ... and I know it's your mother who gives out the corn – but you boys don't seem to have any say at all. It does seem a bit strange ...

Reader 3   So, the next day, Smee persuaded his brother that they ought to go and see Mallorn about this.

Smee: We've been thinking, Mother, we want some more corn today please. Don't we, Frith?

Mallorn   I'm sorry but you know this is all we can have.

Smee   But why?

Mallorn   Because it's only wise. If you want food throughout the year, then we can only have so much each day.

Smee   But we want it all now, in the Winter, when it's cold.

Mallorn   And what are you going to eat in the Spring?

Frith   That's right. Everybody knows you get stomach-ache if you eat the green corn. I think Mother's right.

Smee   Well in that case, we need more warmth. These miserable helpings of corn don't give us the strength to collect firewood even. I tell you what, why don't we cut a few branches off this precious tree ...?

Mallorn   The tree? Never! I've told you the tree must never be touched.

Smee   But why?

Mallorn	Because the tree stands at the centre of our lives. It shades us in the Summer, shelters us in Winter – so you must never touch it! Do you understand?
Reader 4	But Smee's thoughts burned in his mind. He was older now – and by next Summer, he decided, he would take charge. Then the corn would be his.
Reader 5	At last the Summer came.
Smee	Now – Mother, Frith – this year we must store more corn for eating ...
Mallorn	But I thought we'd settled this last year. Half to eat, half to sow.
Frith	Yes, Smee. If we eat more, we won't have enough seed corn for next year, will we?
Smee	No, dear Frith, but if we put more water on the seeds, they'll grow even bigger, won't they ...?
Frith	Yes... but ...
Smee	Then we won't need as many seeds, will we?
Frith	But you'll over-water the corn ...
Smee	Nonsense – don't worry so.
Mallorn	But can't you see? Does your greed blind you to everything, Smee? We work with Nature, not against her. We dare not ... we must not take too much ...
Smee	We've argued enough. It's time for a decision. Well, Frith, whose idea is the best this time?
Frith	Well, yours I suppose, Smee.
Reader 6	So, the next day the golden corn was cut, with only a quarter of it returned to the soil. And the trench from the pool was cut deeper and the water gushed in torrents on to the corn patch.
Reader 1	And, as planned, in the Winter, there was more food for everyone, but the snow still fell and the cold closed in – and the wind bit just as deeply as ever.
Smee	I've never known such cold. It's f ... f ... freezing, and this fire's almost out!
Frith	Well, Mother's out there gathering sticks. Perhaps we should help her.
Smee	Not me. It's cold enough to freeze your blood.
Reader 2	So, neither of them did anything. They just sat there until that sly, tempting voice came back again.
2nd Voice	Smee, Frith. You don't have to go very far for firewood – look up, look around you. There's wood enough for a whole Winter of warmth. The tree! Make it yours. Cut it down. Cut it down!

Smee	Come on, Frith, get an axe.
Frith	No, no – we can't. What about Mother?
Smee	Oh she'll love it when she sees the fire.
Frith	But it's not right, Smee. This tree means so much to us. Think what it gives us – a place of shelter, a place for talking, a place to live ...
Smee	And a place to die, if we don't get warm. Come on, Frith – the axe!
Reader 3	So, Frith just stood there as Smee chopped the tree down, gathered up the branches and threw them on the embers of the old fire.
Smee	Wonderful, wonderful. It's like the warmth of Summer, isn't it Frith?
Reader 4	But before Frith could reply, their mother answered for him.
Mallorn	No, no, stop! Smee? Frith? What have you done?
Reader 5	But it was too late. The tree was dead and gone.
Reader 6	To begin with, everything went according to Smee's plan. There was plenty of corn and firewood. But, when the Spring arrived as usual, this time it was greeted with sadness not joy.
Reader 1	By then, the firewood was all burnt, the grain all gone. The tree was just a circle of ashes and the corn seeds never grew. They had rotted in the over-watered soil. And Smee and Frith knew they had been foolish.
Reader 2	Mallorn hopelessly longed for the tree to grow again. As she lay in the ashes, with her eyes closed, she seemed to hear, in a dream, a voice she knew.
1st Voice	Mallorn, Mallorn. I am the last seed of the tree. I am a gift from the heart of death. I survived the careless hands of mankind, and the cruel tongues of fire. So, this time, heed my words. Tend me, care for me – and all will be well. Remember, I am your life ... tend me ...
Reader 3	And when Mallorn awoke, she was amazed. For just by her head she saw a green shoot – a tiny tree – struggling to push its way up through the ashes.

Ben's flowers

Ben's flowers has connotations of the Easter message, addressing issues of bereavement and regeneration.

It was the worst possible start. Rain pouring the whole journey. Mum and Dad bickering as they tried to keep close behind the furniture van. My sister Jen feeling sick, sitting next to me in the back of the car. And then Ben's accident.

I'd known as soon as I'd heard the squeal of brakes. Someone had left the front door open in all the comings and goings and now Ben was dead. We'd been in our new house for just two hours.

I'd never wanted to move anyway. What's the good of a house if it's on a main road? A busy main road with tanker lorries, like the one that killed Ben.

'You won't hear the traffic through the double-glazed windows,' Dad had said. I didn't need to hear it to know it was there. I'd never forget it was there. It would always be there. But Ben wouldn't.

He had always been around. When Jen and I got home from school he'd meet us at the gate, bounding up, licking our hands. We'd drop our school bags in the porch and take him for a walk. Or rather he'd take us, dragging us behind him as he strained at the lead, eager to reach the field at the back of our old house.

Once there he'd run in huge circles, gradually closing until he was nipping at our heels. We were sheep and he was rounding us up. Then he'd lie panting on the grassy bank at the top of the field, pink tongue bright against black jaws.

'Ben!' I shouted, hearing the squeal of brakes. Panicking with sudden, certain knowledge I raced out of the room. Jen, catching my desperation, ran after me.

The tanker lorry was slewed across the road, front wheels straddling the grass verge. I turned my back to avoid the sight of Ben's crumpled, lifeless body.

Dad pulled me towards him, his arms sheltering me. I struggled to free myself, lashing out with clenched fists, tasting tears, sobbing uncontrollably. Dad held me, talking softly, speaking Ben's name. I was just aware of Mum clutching Jen, their heads buried together.

At last Mum, Jen and I went back inside our new house and Dad went down to the road.

I'd loved my old house, my old street, my old school.

We didn't even get an extra holiday. We moved in the half-term break. Our new school was huge. All concrete and glass with long corridors and shiny plastic tiled floors.

Three hundred children, and I didn't know one of them.

Sometimes we'd had new kids at my old school. You had to be nice to them, show them round, where the toilets were, stuff like that. But nobody could really help them: they had to help themselves.

Some fitted in straightaway. Others took ages. You'd find them crying quietly in the cloakroom at lunch-times. I'd never really thought about it before. New teachers, different rules. Everybody knowing everything and you finding out one thing at a time.

That's what I was thinking about when I heard the squeal of brakes. And then I forgot all about it. I just thought of Ben.

Dad came in looking tired. He cleared his throat and sat on one of the unopened boxes.

'He wouldn't have known anything about it,' he began, 'it would have all been over before he felt anything ...'

'For goodness sake, shut up Dad,' I thought. 'How do you know what Ben felt?' Tears began welling up. I wasn't listening to Dad anymore. He was talking and rummaging in the boxes like a mad thing. Then he was holding something in front of my face. Spread in the palms of his hands were some wizened brown bulbs. Like onions. And he was still talking.

'I'll get the car out and we'll go back to our old house.'

'Back to our old house?'

If only we could go back to this morning. I'd hold Ben so tight ...

'And we'll plant them in the field. On that grassy bank where you used to play.'

What was he talking about? Plant bulbs in a field?

Dad went into the field on his own. We waited in the car until he'd got the unpleasant business over, then trudged across the wet grass to join him. We all scraped up clumps of grass and pressed the bulbs into the soft earth beneath. We worked silently. I still didn't really understand why we were there.

That night in my bedroom I counted cracks in the ceiling. Cars, sounding like supercharged bees, buzzed constantly along the road outside.

Jen sat on my bed. For a girl she didn't cry much.

'It can only get better, Simon,' she said.

In the morning I'd get up early and walk down to look at the new school. On my own.

It was Spring when we went back to our old house. The new people had changed the garden. They'd turfed our vegetable plot and put a rotary clothes line in the middle.

Worse still they'd put up a high fence out the back. It wasn't the same anymore. I bet they'd scraped off my wallpaper and taken down my bookshelves.

As soon as we got to the field I knew what Dad had meant.

We could see the yellow trumpeted flowers from the gate. They were Ben's flowers.

And we could come back and see them every year.

Ian Addis

Pesach

Pesach, or **Passover**, is the Jewish festival of freedom, celebrating the exodus of the Israelites from captivity in Egypt (Exodus chapters 5–7).

The Jews were required to leave Egypt so rapidly that there was no time to bake bread in the traditional way, using leaven to make the dough rise. The event is commemorated in one of the main features of the festival which is also known as 'the feast of the unleavened bread'. In the words of Exodus 34:18

> *The feast of the unleavened bread shalt thou keep.*
> *Seven days thou shalt eat unleavened bread, as I*
> *commanded thee ...*

On the eve of the festival, Jews conduct a search of their homes to remove and ritually destroy any hametz – yeast or any other rising agent. This is more than just symbolic of the hasty flight from Egypt, it also represents the need to rid their lives of pride and live with greater humility. Throughout Pesach, Jews eat **matzah**, which is unleavened bread, rather like a flat cracker biscuit.

A family ceremony, known as seder, takes place on the first two evenings of the festival. During the service, the story of the exodus is related from the Haggadah or 'guidebook to the Passover'. A meal is held, comprising a variety of foods, each significant in reinforcing understanding of the occasion:

A roasted shankbone of lamb commemorates the sacrifice made in olden times. Bitter herbs (horseradish) remind Jews of the harshness of slavery. Haroset (mixed nuts, apple and cinnamon) represents the mortar used by the workgangs who built the great monuments to the Pharaohs. Karpas (parsley) is a symbol of spring-time and hope. Salt water is for the tears shed by the slaves, and to represent the crossing of the Red Sea. Roasted egg is a traditional festival offering at the temple in Jerusalem. Four cups of wine are a reminder of the four promises made by God to redeem Israel. Finally, a plate of **matzot** (unleavened bread) is held up, recalling the dramatic flight from Egypt. This is accompanied by words from the Haggadah.

There are many links between the Jewish Pesach and the Christian spring festival. Jesus was crucified during the Feast of the Passover and the first Christians, who were all Jews, turned the occasion into the celebration of Easter. And in many European languages, the name for Easter is derived from the Hebrew word Pesach; e. g. Danish = Paaska, Italian = Pasqua, Swedish = Pask, Welsh = Pasg.

Ramadan and Id-Ul-Fitr

The Muslim festival of **Id-Ul-Fitr** marks the end of Ramadan, a month of fasting. Like Easter, its precise date varies from year to year, but it always takes place on the first day of the tenth month in the Muslim calendar.

There are similarities between Ramadan, the time when Muhammad went alone up into the hills above Makkah in order to fast and meditate, and the 40 days and nights spent by Jesus in the wilderness. It was during Ramadan that Muhammad received the first of his revelations from Allah, recorded later in the Qur'an. This is commemorated on the 27th day of Ramadan by a special 'Night of Power' called Laylat-Ul-Qadr.

Throughout the month of Ramadan, all adult Muslims (over the age of 12 and in good health) abstain from food and drink during the hours of daylight. The purpose of the fast is to enable the rich to experience the rigours of poverty, and to establish expectations of behaviour for the rest of the year.

The morning of Id-Ul-Fitr begins with a ceremony in the mosque, and worshippers wear new or special clothes as a symbol of re-generation. Families then gather to celebrate with a special meal, Id greetings cards are exchanged, and children receive presents from relatives and friends. Donations are also made to the poor and needy.

Activities

There are opportunities for a range of cross-curricular activities associated with the spring-time festivals detailed above.

Easter

Design and build an **Easter garden** depicting the scene at Calvary, to provide a focal point in the classroom, foyer or assembly hall.
Make **Easter biscuits**, incorporating aspects of science, language, maths and design technology as children measure and mix ingredients.

Class or school competitions involving hard-boiled or blown eggs, can provide a popular stimulus. The eggs can be decorated using paints or felt tips, or extended by adding pieces of card, beads, buttons or seeds to create animals or people. Another 'eggtivity', using more sophisticated design technology skills is the **Humpty Dumpty** competition. Children are required to devise a means of protecting their raw egg from breakage when dropped from a uniform height of two metres so that the test is fair. Any method is acceptable – insulation, parachute, a protective frame – within agreed guidelines.

Egg tangrams, for conversion into bird patterns, make appropriate designs for Easter cards.

From Peak Mathematics, *Nelson*

Imaginatively designed containers – a hot air balloon, a horse and carriage, a lorry or basket to hold a chocolate-cream filled egg – make ideal presents for relatives.

Children will enjoy incubating eggs and monitoring their progress in an egg diary.

Easter bonnets, designed from card and decorated with crepe ribbons provide a colourful feature of an Easter parade.

Younger children will enjoy making **pom-pom chicks** from short lengths of wool.

Spring flowers make perfect life-drawing subjects and are excellent for **Easter card designs**. Aquarelle painting pencils offer a range of delicate shades ideally suited for the primrose, polyanthus, daffodil, narcissus, snowdrop or violet.

Large-scale class or school cards can be presented to local 'personalities' such as the site supervisor, dinner supervisor or lollipop lady, or sent to the children's ward at the local hospital.

Pesach

Prepare Pesach food, and hold a class feast. The following is a recipe for haroset.

Ingredients:

one small apple peeled and cored
a few stoned dates
a few seedless raisins
one teaspoon of candied peel
a few peeled almonds
cinnamon to taste

Method:

Chop or mince the ingredients very finely, add cinnamon and moisten with a little apple juice.

Id-Ul-Fitr

Making Id greetings cards (based on patterns and designs from Islamic art) offers an excellent design and technology activity.

The wide variety of festival food includes Dimer Pita, from this simple Bengali recipe.

Dimer pita

Ingredients:
100g (4 oz) rice flour
100g (4 oz) sugar
two small eggs
Pinch of salt

Method:

Mix flour, sugar and salt together.

Beat the eggs and add very gradually to the flour mixture until it handles like dough. If too wet add a little more flour.

Roll it out gently to about 1/2 cm thickness – no thinner.

Cut it into shapes with biscuit cutters or a knife or make some little balls.

Fry it in fairly deep vegetable oil in a chip pan until light golden on both sides. The little biscuits will puff up in the hot oil. Keep turning them and make sure they remain well covered in oil. This takes about four to five minutes. This amount will make about two dozen small biscuity cakes.

Chapter 11

A Place in the Sun

Try and hold the sunshine
in your hand –
It will slip through your fingers.

Try and catch the sunshine
as you run –
It will slide behind the hill.

But watch,
And you'll find the sunshine –
Hidden in a flower,
Beaming in a smile,
And sparkling like a secret
In your best friend's eyes.

Gaining recognition

The importance of children gaining recognition for a range of qualities, not merely those limited to academic achievement, is vitally important if they are to fulfil a role as caring, tolerant members of tomorrow's society, confident that each has something worthwhile to contribute. Schools should seek to give everyone 'a place in the sun'.

Throughout the school year, children are encouraged to develop and practise a variety of skills, many of which come to fruition during the summer term. While it is important to recognise the achievements of the more gifted, the efforts of those less naturally blessed should also be acknowledged. The material in this section focuses upon both the richly endowed, and those who overcome adversity to achieve a personal goal.

Arthur, the fat boy

In his poem, 'Arthur the fat boy', Gareth Owen relates the story of the perennial loser's eventual triumph.

They said about Arthur: You're too fat.
They said you never can win,
Only make a fool of yourself.
They said: Arthur think again.

But Arthur was sick of the insults
He was tired of all the names
He was fed up with being never asked to play
When they picked their teams for games.

So secretly he went running
In the evenings after tea
Past the allotments down to the old canal
Where he thought no one would see.

And there each night Arthur ran alone
Till his fat pink legs were numb
And the sweat on his face was a river
And his lungs beat like a drum.

He ran past locks and bridges
Where abandoned factories reared
Where the wind on the water called his name
And only the silence jeered.

When finally sports day came around
And Arthur jogged to his place
And the mocking shouts of the jeering crowd
Made the tears course down his face.

But the jeers and the laughter died away
When the starter fired his gun
And a voice rang clear across the field
Just look at that fat boy run.

Two laps from home and Arthur lies fourth
There's a map of pain on his face
And only his rage keeps him running
As he moves into third place.

He inches up on the second boy
The leader's just ten yards ahead
And the voice in the crowd is a roar in his head
And the faces a sea of red.

And Arthur the fat boy sees the tape
And his pride has become a mine
And he scratches with his will for strength there
As his legs swim for the line.

And Arthur the fat boy makes first place
But the sky is upside down
And the finish appears to be moving away
As he falls to his knees on the ground.

He can hear the second boy closing fast
But his legs have turned to lead
And his brain can't hear his will power scream
Through the blizzard in his head.

And though for the first time in his life
He hears the crowd call his name
Arthur lies stranded high and alone
Beached on a rack of pain.

Then a mocking voice rings high and clear
It's a voice he's heard all his life
And the jeering, leering mockery
Twists in his heart like a knife.

And it's anger that sets him moving
Anger that lifts him again
It's anger that pushes his aching legs
Crawling across the line.

And Arthur the fat boy dreams he's in bed
And he clings to his dream in fear
So many cold mornings he's woken to see
His happiness disappear.

And Arthur reluctantly wakens himself
And the world turns like a wheel
And Arthur for the first time in his life
Awakes to a world that's real.

The tooth

This story about Koku and the tropical storm tells of the triumph of will over adversity.

The great white rock towered sixty feet above the sand below. Square topped and sheer it could be seen from all over the island.

People called it The Tooth.

And none knew it better than Koku.

Every day he would join the men-folk of his village to walk the few miles to the sea. But every day he was the last to arrive. Even the old men would pass him.

'Come on Koku,' they said kindly. 'You'll catch no fish again today.'

They meant no harm. It was their little joke. But the boy didn't laugh. By the time Koku reached the shore the canoes were already out of sight.

They would return at dusk. Then he would help to unload the catch, drag the boats back up the beach and stow them safely away for the night. That was his special job. He was always the last to leave, always the last to return to the village. Until then he joined the old men mending nets in the shade of the great rock. Sometimes he would listen to their tales of far-off days, but when he grew bored with the chatter he would gaze out at the sea and wish for the thousandth time that he was riding the giant waves with his father and brothers.

Or he would stare up at The Tooth until he knew every inch of its shiny surface, every crack, every crevice. Countless times Koku had climbed to the very top, stood on its flat peak and waved to his friends in the fishing boats or his mother and sisters in the village. But only in his dreams. Time dragged by that morning. It seemed like an eternity before dozens of tiny specks appeared on the horizon. The canoes were turning, carried ashore on the incoming tide, the freshening wind speeding their passage.

It had been a good catch. The nets were heavy with glistening silver fish.

His brothers were in playful mood.

'And what have you caught today Koku?' one asked as they came ashore.

'Maybe he's caught a cold,' replied another.

'Or a crab in those nets he's been mending.'

Their father frowned.

'Leave him alone,' he said sternly. 'Don't tease ...'

Laughing, the brothers turned away and ran back down to the water to empty the boats.

It was a long time before Koku could begin his final task. Alone on the beach he struggled to upturn the canoes and stack them in the shelter of The Tooth.

The wind was strengthening and becoming chill. Clouds raced each other across the darkening sky. A storm was approaching. Koku hated storms. Usually they would pass harmlessly across the island barely pausing to dampen the villages below.

But occasionally they were in determined mood like gatecrashers at a party wreaking havoc and upset before moving on. Koku grimaced at the thought. Oh yes, Koku hated storms. He looked seaward again. There was no horizon anymore. Clouds and waves had merged into a huge grey wall moving slowly towards the shore.

His job done, Koku turned his back and hurried towards the path through the sand dunes. For a brief moment the air became still. The roar of wind and waves died down. There was silence. The boy sensed that something was wrong. He remembered the story the old men told of a terrible night before his grandfather was born. A night when the angry sea swallowed up the island, leaving only the great rock and the tallest trees standing above the waves.

Koku looked back once more. Slowly, but surely, the wall of water was coming closer. Again he felt the fierce wind beat in his face. Suddenly he knew what he must do. Reaching forward he rummaged amongst the pebbles at the foot of The Tooth. Water was already beginning to trickle between his fingers as he searched. At last he was satisfied. He tucked his find safely inside his belt and stared up at the high rock. The time for dreaming was over. Now he really had to climb.

He'd planned the path so many times before. But he could never have imagined the strength of the wind, or the ache in his shoulders as he pulled himself upwards carefully seeking out every handhold. He'd known pain before. Real pain. For hours he had lain crushed beneath the great tree that had crashed down on his family's hut while the men struggled to lift it from his legs. Now those legs were wasted. Useless. No fishing for him.

He was fit only to mend nets and stack canoes with the old ones. Oh yes, he hated storms.

But this one wouldn't win. Koku had decided.

His arms were strong. He would reach the top and ...

The sound of water interrupted his thoughts.

Glancing down he could see huge waves beating against the rock, creeping ever higher up the beach.

Locking his fingers inside a tiny crevice, he heaved his heavy legs higher up the rock face. He must reach the top and warn the village. Let them know of the danger. Give them time to reach safety.

But it was hard. The rock was greasy from the driving rain and his legs were a dead weight.

Once more he heard his brothers' mocking words – 'What did you catch today Koku, a cold?' – as he pulled himself nearer to The Tooth's flat summit. The beach was already submerged. Water was climbing the dunes. Soon it would find the path to the village. One last heave took Koku to the top. There was barely time to pause for breath. Then the boy reached inside his belt, took the huge conch shell and blew hard and long. A tuneless wail echoed around the rock.

From his perch high on the peak Koku could see tiny figures running from their huts and staring seawards. He blew into the shell once more and waved in desperation. They understood. In minutes the clearing was filled with people clutching bundles, carrying babies. Soon they would reach the safety of the huts built high in the treetops.

His work done, Koku lay exhausted on the flat rock top. By morning the unwelcome visitor would have left the island. Slowly the waters would recede and he would be able to climb down the rock. Once more he would help the old men mend nets and stack canoes when the boats returned from the sea laden with fish.

And Koku knew that no-one would laugh at him. Ever again.

Charles Marlow

ADDITIONAL RESOURCES:

Helen Keller, Great Lives Series, Wayland
The One and Only Delgado Cheese, a tale of talent, fame and friendship, by Bob Hartman, Lion.

Carla's gift

The school concert gives children an opportunity to demonstrate their individual and collective talents, although sometimes the occasion is fraught with unexpected problems.

When Mr Stanger left we gave him a garden lounger, a teasmade and a big clap in the hall.

After the Easter holiday there was a new teacher playing the piano in the morning assembly. This one had long blonde braided hair, a dress down to her ankles and rows of wooden beads. The music was different too. They were the same old tunes, but instead of sounding tired like before, they sort of bounced. Everyone joined in. Even the teachers. Normally they moaned at us for not singing, but just hid their faces behind their hymn books.

The new music teacher was called Mrs Parker. After a few weeks she said she was starting a school choir. We had to go to her room at playtime if we wanted to join.

'You've got two choices' she said, when some of the boys started messing about. 'You can stay, or you can go. If you stay, you behave yourselves. If you go, you don't come back. Take your pick!'

She spoke quietly, but I knew she meant it. Some went. Kenny Gray, Philip Spiers, Colin Dix. Good riddance, they were creeps. The rest stayed. And they behaved themselves. Mrs Parker looked soft, but she could chill you with a stare. Just a look spoke a hundred words.

When I told my mum I was joining the choir she said 'Oh, and how long will that last I wonder?'

I was a great joiner. The trouble was, I was an even greater leaver. I waited for it. I knew what was coming.

'You've still got a Brownie uniform up in the wardrobe. Brand new. Only worn twice.'

That was only a start.

'And what about you and your horse riding? Three times you went. Nearly landed us with buying a pair of jodhpurs and a riding hat.' I told her about Mrs Parker. 'I've heard about her from Lesley Walker's mum at work. All airy fairy, arty crafty she sounds. You'll soon get tired of her.'

But I didn't. It was great in the choir. We were singing songs from *Cats* in the Schools' Music Festival in June. The first time I'd been in a concert in my life.

The trouble was, that was when the trouble started.

'You've got a gift, Carla' Mrs Parker had said during practice one lunchtime. That's all. Well, what would you think if someone said that? I thought I'd got a prize. Perhaps she was going to give me a couple of team points. That's what Katy Clark thought.

'That makes a change' she sneered, 'you getting team points.' She can be really nasty, Katy Clark can. But she was right. I hardly ever won any team points.

I thought about the choir practice for the hundredth time. We were singing one of the festival songs, 'Memory'. Mrs Parker suddenly said,

'Quiet, everyone – except Carla.'

I sang on, on my own to the end of the verse. That's when she said I'd got the gift.

I never heard Mr Garfield's question. Everywhere had gone quiet. I looked round the room and they were all looking at me.

'Well, Carla. We're waiting.'

I didn't know what he was talking about.

'No idea, have you? Where were you, girl? You'd better wake your ideas up, young lady. They'll soon bring you down to earth at Secondary School ...'

He went on and on. I never did find out what the question was.

When the bell went at a quarter to four I was changing my shoes in the cloakroom. Mrs Parker called me.

'Carla. Just a minute, please.'

This was it. My gift at last. I went across to the door.

'I'd like you to do something special for the Music Festival.'

That wasn't what I expected.

'I thought you might sing a solo. The verse from "Memory" you sang today.'

That was all. Nothing else. That was my gift? It was more like a punishment. To stand up in front of all those people. On my own. And sing. My knees started to tremble right there in the doorway.

'Think about it, Carla. There's no hurry. Tell me tomorrow.'

Some girls from my class were listening.

'Who's gonna be a superstar then? Carla Minogue.'

I laughed with them but I was still dead nervous.

That night I dreamt about Mrs Parker. Only she wasn't Mrs Parker. Her face was like a cat. Whiskered and grinning.

'You've got a gift' she purred from on top of the piano. And then she started to laugh. Louder and louder. I woke up, all of a sweat. My alarm clock showed twelve. 'Midnight. Not a sound from the pavement.' Eventually I dropped off to sleep again.

The next day I told her I would. Sing the solo that is. She just said 'better get plenty of practice, then.'

That was easier said than done in our house. I met my mum

going out of the gate as I arrived home from school that afternoon.

'Bye, love' she said. 'Your dinner's the one on the little plate. See you in the morning.'

She was off to stack shelves at Superstore. I'd be asleep by the time she got back. No time to tell her my news. Three plates sat on the kitchen table. Like in the three bears. A little plate. That was mine. A medium-sized plate. That was my brother Derek's. He wasn't home from Tech. yet. You knew when he was in from halfway down the street. Heavy metal music blaring out of every window. And a great big plate. That was my dad's. He was still at work as usual. If he was in, it would be the telly, turned up full blast. When they were both in it was like a madhouse. *Iron Maiden* upstairs. *Coronation Street* downstairs. How could I practise my solo amongst that? But so far this evening, I was on my own. I went into the living room with my songsheet, to make the most of the peace and quiet.

'Hello, Carla, I've been waiting for you. Can you read the paper to me before the others get back?'

Oh no! Gran was here. I'd forgotten it was Thursday. She always came to visit on Thursdays and I always had to read her the evening paper. From cover to cover. It was hard work. Not only couldn't she see too well, she was as deaf as a post.

'Course I can, Gran' I said, between gritted teeth, and picked up the *Telegraph* from the table.

'Memory loss causes concert chaos' I began. That wasn't fair. There was no chance to practise after that.

The next day I told Dad about the music festival.

'Will you and Mum be able to come?' I asked.

'I'd love to, Carla, but it depends on work. We're up to our eyes at the garage now. Looks like we'll be working late most nights.' He saw the disappointment in my face. 'But I'll try. I promise.'

My mum wasn't sure either. 'A Tuesday night. That's a bad night, Carla. Nobody wants to swap shifts on a Tuesday. But I'll try. Promise.'

'Mrs Parker says I've got a gift' I told my mum that evening.

'I'd fancy a gift' she said. 'One of these genies that pop out of the magic lamp at the pantomime. Perhaps he'd be good at washing and ironing and hoovering and cooking ...'

'I know you're singing solo. Make sure it's so low I can't hear it.' That from my brother, whose music rocked the ceiling and shook the bedroom walls. Was anyone interested?

Mrs Parker spoke to me at school the next day. 'You'll be wanting tickets for the Festival I suppose?' she asked. How could I tell her I didn't think my mum and dad could go?

'Yes please, Mrs Parker. Two I think.'

'You've left it late, Carla. They've nearly all gone. But as you're a bit special you can have mine. Two reserved places. Front row of the balcony. How's that?'

When I blushed Mrs Parker got the wrong idea.

'It's not favouritism, Carla. Don't think that. I always like to sit with the choir so I don't need any tickets. And you are singing a solo.'

On the afternoon of the Festival, we had to stay a bit later for a last minute practice. When I got home I half expected that Mum would still be there. That she'd managed to change her shift at work. But the house was empty. My dinner stood by the microwave. A new blouse and clean pair of white socks lay on a chair in my bedroom. I read through the words for the thousandth time.

The Festival was held in a chapel in town and we had to catch a coach at the school gates at half past six. As we filed into the hall the seats on the balcony were beginning to fill up. There was no sign of my mum or dad. At seven o'clock the conductor rapped the lectern with his stick. Everyone stopped chattering and fidgeting and stood up. The guests of honour were arriving. We looked towards the balcony as the Mayor and Mayoress took their places, all poshed up in their robes and chains. Next to them were two empty seats. The spaces yawned like gaping holes in a row of shining teeth. My mum and dad's seats.

At last it was time for our item. Mrs Parker looked along the row and smiled.

'OK. Let's go' she whispered, and led the way to the stage at the front. The words flitted around in my mind like birds in a cage. They wouldn't keep still. Fancy calling the song 'Memory'. Mrs Parker waited for us to sort ourselves out in the special order and then began to play the introduction. For the first time I dared to look up at the audience. I had to blink and look again. They were there. My dad, in his greasy overalls, was standing aside letting mum sit down next to the Mayoress. She was still wearing her Superstore smock, but I didn't care.

I'd got my gift at last.

And once I began to sing, the little lump in the back of my throat disappeared completely.

Ian Addis

Activities

Alternative sports days

Many schools have extended the traditional sports day, with its emphasis on fastest, highest, longest, to accommodate a variety of alternative events catering for the less athletic. Children can be engaged in organising these alternative sports days, planning events, drawing up a programme, collecting and setting out equipment, making 'medals' etc.

Class Olympics

Another interesting cross-curricular project for the final weeks of the summer term is the Class Olympics. Children are divided into teams, each named after a fictitious country, for which they must design a national flag (and possibly an anthem based on a simple musical phrase). They then have responsibility for devising table-top games, inventing a scoring and recording system, ensuring that activities are judged fairly, organising medal ceremonies and reporting events for the 'media'.

In an Olympic year, of course, the real games can provide a special focus, perhaps coinciding with the school's version.

Reception children with home-made javelins

Open days

Open days, when the school displays a range of activities and projects reflecting work completed throughout the year, provide an excellent 'showcase' to point up achievement. They also provide parents with a valuable opportunity to witness progression through the age-groups by examining children's work at various levels.

To assist children in developing a sense of ownership for the occasion, it is important to involve them in its organisation and execution. Special invitations can be designed and delivered to parents, governors etc. Welcome notices might be posted around the building Children can prepare 'guidebooks' for visitors to use on their tour around the school, ensuring that special points of interest are visited, and classroom quizzes requiring visitors to seek out information from the work displayed. Explanatory audiotapes can be prepared, providing details relating to class projects. Many schools have 'workshop' sessions in progress, in which children demonstrate their skills across the curriculum. Design technology projects provide particularly exciting display possibilities.

Achievement board

An achievement board, providing evidence of community involvement, charity work, certificates, trophies, newspaper reports and photographs of school events etc., accumulated during the year, can be displayed in a prominent place.

Many teachers use a 'best board', giving esteem to individual children by recognising the improved quality of their work, exemplary behaviour, good manners, or a specific contribution to class or school life. Records of achievement, including self-appraisal by pupils, can follow the child through the school, monitoring progress and boosting self esteem.

Hold fast to dreams,
For if dreams die
Life is a broken-winged bird
That cannot fly.

Hold fast to dreams
For when dreams go
Life is a barren field
Frozen with snow.

Chapter 12

One More Step

A project using the theme of 'journeys' provides scope for incorporating a range of activities in the summer term. Not only do many children enjoy class visits to places of interest – zoos, museums, farms, bird sanctuaries – but some have opportunities for residential experience, often in an unfamiliar environment.

This chapter examines how the Christian word was spread. It also looks at pilgrimages, expeditions and explorations, travels around the school and its environs, class outings and residential visits, and it considers the implications for pupils about to step out on the next stage of their educational journey.

Like Easter, the Christian festival of **Whitsun** (which takes place 50 days later), has its origins in a Jewish celebration. The Apostles were gathered in Jerusalem for the Feast of Pentecost (a day of thanksgiving for the first fruits of the harvest) and to commemorate the receiving of the Ten Commandments by Moses on Mount Sinai (Acts 2: 1 – 4).

> *And when the feast of Pentecost was fully come, they were all with one accord in one place. And suddenly there came a sound from heaven as of a rushing mighty wind, and it filled all the houses where they were sitting. And there appeared unto them cloven tongues like as of fire, and it sat upon each of them. And they were all filled with the Holy Ghost, and began to speak with other tongues, as the spirit gave them utterance.*

Fired with evangelical zeal, the Apostles sought to spread the 'good news' throughout the world, and the birth of the Christian Church is often said to date from that first Whitsun.

The missionary journeys of St Paul are recounted in Acts chapters 13–28.

Many stories are told of the **coming of Christianity to Britain**. One story maintains that St Peter himself established the Church here, another attributes the founding to St Paul, while the most familiar version tells how Joseph of Arimathea came to Somerset in the course of his trading voyages, and built the first Christian Church on the summit of the holy hill at Glastonbury. Alongside the primitive building, he planted a piece of the crown of thorns from Christ's crucifixion. A tree, grown from this thorn cutting, flowered on Christmas Day in commemoration of the birth of Jesus.

Described as the 'cradle of Christianity', Glastonbury also features in the Arthurian legend of the Quest for the Holy Grail. The story of Arthur (a fifth century British tribal chief famous for resisting the invading Angles and Saxons) tells how the king despatched his knights on a mission to search for the chalice used by Christ at the Last Supper and reputedly brought to England by Joseph of Arimathea.

These stories were written long after their supposed date, but, whatever doubts exist about their authenticity, Glastonbury was an important centre of early Christianity, its abbey said to have been founded in AD 700 on the site of the original church building.

During the Roman occupation, Christianity thrived most vigorously in those parts of Britain ruled by the Celts. The first of the Celtic saints was **Ninian**, son of a tribal chief, who was raised a Christian and in the last years of the fourth century made a pilgrimage to Rome from his home in Galloway on the Solway Firth. There he attracted the attention of Pope Siricius, who consecrated him a bishop before sending him back to Scotland with a mission to convert his countrymen.

On his return, Ninian established a new monastery at Whithorn, constructed with the help of stone-masons from Tours, whose work he had admired on his journey through France. The whitewashed stone building was completed in AD 397 and dedicated to Saint Martin. Although the monastery was destroyed long ago, a ruined priory remains to mark the place, and a sea cave with a rough cross carved on its walls, where Ninian spent hours in prayer and contemplation, still survives.

Famous journeys by early British Christians include those of **Saint Patrick** from Antrim in Northern Ireland to Auxerre in AD 405; **Saint Columba** from Donegal to Iona in AD 563; **Saint Aidan** from Iona to Lindisfarne in AD 635; and **Benedict Biscop** and **Saint Wilfred** from Northumbria to Rome in AD 653. Benedict returned a further five times to Rome which was such a hazardous venture at that time that travellers frequently made their wills before setting out.

One British Christian, **Winfrid (later Saint Boniface)** became a missionary to continental Europe, travelling from his monastery at Nursling, near Southampton, to Utrecht in AD 718. He later worked in Germany, establishing monasteries as centres and guardians of the Christian faith, before returning to Frisia, where he was murdered by raiders in AD 754.

Perhaps the best known of the missionaries who travelled to Britain during this early period is **Saint Augustine**. Encouraged by Pope Gregory, he landed on the Isle of Thanet in the summer of AD 597, where he was introduced to Ethelbert, the King of Kent. Ethelbert's wife, Bertha, already worshipped at a small church in Canterbury, and in June, shortly after Augustine's arrival, the King was baptised in the Christian faith.

Appointed Archbishop of Canterbury, Augustine was given the task of unifying the Christian Church in Britain. Hostility from the Celts was a major obstacle in the north and west, and he decided to concentrate his efforts in the south-east, using Canterbury as a base, under the patronage of the friendly Ethelred. In the year before his death in AD 605, Augustine established the second English Bishopric at Rochester and later that same year Mellitus was consecrated Bishop of the East Saxons, with his seat at London.

ADDITIONAL RESOURCES:

The Early Christians in Britain, Dodd and Heritage, Longman

Journeys to places considered sacred by 'believers' are known as **pilgrimages. Muslims** are expected to travel to Makkah, the birthplace of Muhammad, at least once during their lifetime. Every year, during the twelfth month, known as Dhu I-Hijjah, about two million Muslims make the Hajj, or chief pilgrimage, following the traditional route to the courtyard of the Great Mosque in Makkah. In the middle of the courtyard stands the Ka'bah, a small building which houses the sacred Black Stone, believed by Muslims to have been given to Ibrahim by Allah 4,000 years ago.The visit requires a ritual kissing of the stone. By the tenth day of Dhu I-Hijjah, the pilgrims will have travelled the eight kilometres to Mina and its three stone pillars, said to mark the spot where Ishmael was tempted by the devil to disobey his father Ibrahim. The travellers collect 49 pebbles to throw at the pillars as a reminder of the temptations they must face in their own lives and of the need to oppose all evil and do Allah's will. The action leads into the celebration of Id-Ul-Adha which ends the pilgrimage.

In medieval times, parties of **Christian pilgrims** travelled to pay homage at the shrines of saints, many of whom were located in the great cathedral cities across Europe. The story of one such group journeying to the shrine of Saint Thomas à Becket, the Archbishop of Canterbury murdered in 1170, is told in Geoffrey Chaucer's *Canterbury Tales*. Chaucer's pilgrims, who represent a cross-section of contemporary society, provide a beautifully-drawn impression of fourteenth century England. Begun in about 1386 and never completed, the work contains 23 tales ranging from the highly moralistic to the frivolous and bawdy, and is considered one of the masterpieces of English literature.

Another well-known story of pilgrimage is *The Pilgrim's Progress*, written by John Bunyan in 1675 while he was a prisoner of conscience in Bedford Gaol. The book has since been translated into over a hundred languages. The allegorical story, told as in a dream, describes Christian's hazardous journey from the City of Destruction to the Celestial City in search of salvation.

During his lengthy imprisonment as a hostage in Beirut, the Archbishop of Canterbury's Middle-Eastern envoy, Terry Waite, received a postcard from a well-wisher in England. It depicted John Bunyan in Bedford Gaol. On his eventual release from captivity, Terry Waite made reference to the strength and inspiration he drew from the picture.

A study of **exploratory journeys** offers excellent cross-curricular opportunities for children across the primary range. Stories of pioneering expeditions can provide an appropriate introduction to the theme of journeys. A list of possible subjects is given below.

AD 900	Vikings visit Greenland
1000	Leif Ericson discovers Labrador and Newfoundland
1271–95	The journeys of Marco Polo
1487–88	Bartholomeu Diaz rounds Cape of Good Hope into the Indian Ocean
1492	Christopher Columbus discovers the West Indies
1497–98	John and Sebastian Cabot reach Greenland and the shores of Newfoundland and Nova Scotia
1498	Vasco da Gama arrives in Calicut
1499–1500	Vespucci explores the north-east coast of South America
1500	Cabral lands in Brazil
1513	Balboa looks upon the Pacific after crossing the Isthmus of Panama
1519–25	Cortez explores and conquers Mexico
1520	Magellan sails into the Pacific from the Atlantic and completes the first circumnavigation of the world
1524–38	Pizarro explores north-west South America and conquers Peru
1534–36	Cartier explores the Gulf of St Lawrence as far as Montreal
1577–80	Drake sails round the world
1610–11	Hudson discovers Hudson Bay
1769–79	Cook voyages to Australia, New Zealand, Hawaii
1795–1805	Mungo Park reaches the River Niger
1849–73	Livingstone travels into the heart of Africa
1856–59	Burton and Speke attempt to discover the source of the Nile
1858	Speke discovers Lake Victoria
1874	Stanley explores the Congo River from source to mouth
1888–95	Nanson makes first crossing of Greenland
1909	Peary reaches the North Pole (6 April)
1911	Amundsen reaches the South Pole (16 December)
1961	Gagarin makes first flight into space
1969	Armstrong becomes the first man to walk on the Moon

(Brief and concise accounts can be found in *Famous Explorers*, MacDonald Educational 1969, and comprehensive biographies have been compiled on the lives of most leading explorers. Among other useful publications are *Voyages of Discovery*, by Crone and Kendall, Wayland 1970, and *Antarctica: Land of Frozen Time*, by R A Caras, Philadelphia and New York 1962.

The race to the South Pole

One example of courage, adventure and perseverance is the story of Captain Robert Falcon Scott.

In January 1911, the Norwegian explorer Roald Amundsen set up his Antarctic base camp on the Bay of Whales. That same month, on the opposite side of the Ross Ice Shelf, Captain Robert Scott had established his base camp on McMurdo Sound. The scene was set for one of the most dramatic races of all time. A race across the polar ice to the South Pole.

After setting up a number of supply depots, Amundsen had begun his pole-ward dash on 19 October during the brief Antarctic spring. Everything went so much to plan that the expedition seemed less like an adventure than an organised tour. At 3 p.m. on 14 December the South Pole was reached without mishap, and the return journey to the home base completed on 25 January 1912. The round trip had taken just 99 days.

In contrast, Scott's party had an arduous outward journey. By the time the dreaded Beardmore Glacier was reached, all the Siberian ponies and dogs, on whom they had relied to transport both men and supplies across the ice, were dead and the men had to pull the sledges themselves. Eleven miles from the Pole, they came upon a black flag, sledge and ski tracks and the marks of many dogs in the snow. Amundsen had been there before them. That night, Scott wrote in his diary,

'It is a terrible disappointment, and I am sorry for my loyal companions. Many thoughts come and much discussion have we had. Tomorrow we must march on the Pole and then hasten home with all the speed we can compass. All the daydreams must go; it will be a wearisome return.'

The next day – 17 January 1912 – Scott reached the South Pole. There he found a tent flying the Norwegian flag, and inside, a letter from Amundsen dated 14 December. Progress on the return trek was pitifully slow. Hampered by hunger, cold and fatigue, the party struggled on. Captain Oates, severely frostbitten, realised that his slow progress had become a burden to the others and begged to be left behind. Neither Scott nor his other companions, Wilson and Bowers, would consider his request.

By the middle of March, Oates' condition had worsened and he was now no more than a liability. He knew that to continue pulling him on the sledge would put his companions' lives in jeopardy, and one morning as they huddled in their tent with a blizzard raging outside, he struggled to his feet, saying,

'I am just going outside and may be some time.'

Then he stumbled through the flap and was lost forever in the swirling whiteness.

The expedition ended just 11 miles from the plentiful supplies of food and fuel stored at One Ton Camp. A blizzard had halted their progress, and the three were confined to their tent, growing weaker by the hour. On 29 March Scott wrote the final entry in his diary,

'Outside the door of the tent it remains a scene of whirling drift. I do not think we can hope for better things now. We shall stick it out to the end, but we are getting weaker, of course, and the end cannot be far. It seems a pity, but I do not think I can write more.

R. Scott

For God's sake look after our people.'

The next November a search party found the almost buried tent and the bodies of Scott and his companions. Their belongings were removed, but the men were allowed to remain where they lay.

And then there are school 'expeditions'.

Stone Moses

I hate school trips. At least the travelling bit. I always feel sick, squashed three to a seat on the bus. It doesn't matter what I do. Eat breakfast, eat no breakfast, take a tablet, don't take a tablet, sit at the front, sit at the back, sit on a newspaper, suck a mint, I always feel ill. The bus has only to move to the end of the street and I begin to get that horrible queasy feeling in my tummy. And I want to get off. But this time there was something else. Another reason for not wanting to go.

'Next week we're going on a field trip to Sefton Underwood,' Mr Coleman had said. 'As part of our History topic.'

That sounded alright. If the weather was kind it would be better than sitting in the classroom all day, I thought. Apart from the journey, of course.

'Are we going by coach, Mr Coleman?'

Alison Draper asked the obvious question. The teacher gave the obvious answer.

'Unless you fancy walking, Alison', he said. 'It's about 40 miles as the crow flies.'

'She could fly then,' Nathan Betts shouted.

He's quick, he is. It wasn't all that funny, but everyone laughed. The lesson had been dead boring and we were glad of a break. Mr Coleman raised his voice.

'Alright, joke over. Settle down. Listen!'

The room gradually went quiet as he spelt out the plans for the visit, but he lost me at the castle ruins. My mind was drifting out of the window by then.

When I mentioned the trip to Gran, however, she was fascinated and couldn't stop talking about it. Apparently she'd lived at Sefton Underwood when she was a little girl. She filled my head with so much information I became even more confused. But one thing she told me stood out clearly.

'Be sure to look out for Stone Moses. It's the statue of an old man with flowing hair and a long beard, holding a stick, standing in the middle of the pond in the village green. Sometimes, during the summer we used to paddle through the shallow water, climb on him, and make a wish. People said that if he smiled at you, the wish would come true.'

I told Mr Coleman the next day. I thought he'd be pleased, but he listened until I'd finished and then looked seriously at me. He didn't say anything at first. I think he was wondering if I was winding him up. He still looked serious. The class were quiet, guessing something must be wrong and at last he spoke.

'Sorry Gary, but you must have the wrong village.'

Some people began to giggle, softly. I could hear them. I should have kept quiet but I was angry. Mr Coleman didn't believe me. Worse still, he didn't believe my gran.

'She used to live there when she was a little girl,' I persisted.

Mr Coleman shook his head.

'No, Gary. It's a lovely story but I visited the village last Saturday and I can assure you that there's no statue there.'

I took some stick after that. Small wonder I was dreading the trip.

I considered being ill that morning but I knew I'd got to go. I hadn't dared break the bad news about the statue to Gran, because she'd spoken of little else since. She was certainly more excited about the visit than I was.

'I haven't been back for a good ten years,' she said. 'I'd love to see old Stone Moses again.'

I packed my sandwiches, took a travel pill and put on my new anorak to cheer myself up.

'You're not wearing that!'

'Oh Mum, please.'

'You'll lose it'.

How could she think that? My new coat. No way.

'I won't Mum, I promise'.

When she gave in, I thought perhaps the day wouldn't turn out too badly after all.

We trailed around the village all morning. Mr Coleman was right about the pond. It was covered in thick green slime, a couple of tired looking ducks paddled on the edge, but there was no statue in the middle. No one said anything. They didn't need to. Gary had got it wrong again. I stared out across the murky water and made a wish, just like Gran had done. We finished up at the church. The vicar met us outside and led the way to the great wooden door.

'I'm afraid we have to keep it locked. Even churches aren't safe these days.' Mr Coleman smiled.

'No wonder I couldn't get in when I came to look round last weekend,' he said. We took off our coats and sat down in the pews facing the front while the vicar began his talk.

'You're sitting in the people's part of the church,' he said. 'Look at the ceiling. The shape of the wooden beams. Does it remind you of anything? That's right, it's a bit like the hull of a ship isn't it? And what do we call a large collection of ships? Come on, think... no, not a fleet. Good try, but think again. That's it ... a navy, and we call this part of the church the nave ...'

He went on and on. Next we had the guided tour of the building. The usual things. The font, the pulpit, the brasses, the pillars ... and then the statue. It was standing tall and proud in the corner.

'Our star attraction,' said the vicar. 'But does anyone know who it is?'

Mr Coleman looked at me.

'Gary does,' he said with a grin.

'It's Moses,' I replied. 'Stone Moses.'

I couldn't keep the triumph out of my voice.

'That's right,' said the vicar. 'Clever boy! It's a strange story. For years the statue stood in the middle of the village pond, until one stormy night a couple of years ago he suddenly toppled over into the water. No one knew why. So we lifted him out and brought him into the church for safe keeping.'

As we left the building, I took one last look at the statue. And I'm sure he was smiling. So was I, all the way back to school. For the first time, I didn't feel sick. Not even a twinge. Mr Coleman leaned over my shoulder.

'Well Gary, I'm sorry. I was wrong. You can tell your gran her statue's safe and sound after all.'

I couldn't wait. I raced home, full of excitement, full of myself. Mum was in the kitchen.

'Gary,' she said. 'I knew it.'

For a moment I wondered how she could possibly know. And then I realised. My coat! My new coat! I'd left it in the church.

Ian Addis

Activities

Much of this chapter can be adapted to provide a range of cross-curricular activities. The journeys of the early Christian missionaries and explorers can be recorded on large-scale maps; a time-line can be displayed, promoting an understanding of chronology, with appropriate drawings or paintings of the personalities and models of their craft; many of the stories can easily be adapted for dramatisation and shared with the school community during assembly.

Journeys in and around school

Towards the end of the summer term many schools arrange visits for new entrants due to be admitted in September. The induction programme often includes 'journeys' around the school building and its environs to familiarise the children with their new surroundings.

At Key Stage 1, teachers can develop the theme in a variety of ways. Younger classes will enjoy devising 'imaginary journeys', perhaps starting by accompanying Janet and John Ahlberg's 'Jolly Postman' on his round, recreating the voyage by the 'Owl and the Pussycat', following the runaway gingerbread man or mapping Jack's ascent of the beanstalk. Children can then plot their own journeys to school, improving language skills through references to 'street furniture' and developing road safety awareness by identifying potential 'danger' spots en-route.

Teachers might introduce a science strand through work on the senses eg a 'listening' walk, where children visit different locations around the school and record the variety of sounds heard. Such walks could be used to promote language skills, eg practising phonics by identifying objects with specified initial letter sounds, or to reinforce maths concepts, such as recognising common 2-D or 3-D shapes in and around the building – square, rectangular or hexagonal paving slabs, a triangular apex, circular car tyres etc. The theme can be continued in PE where children can explore different ways of 'travelling', following prescribed or random routes, observing pre-conditions or initiating their own rules.

ADDITIONAL RESOURCES:

Mr Bear's Journey, by Chizuko Kuratomi (Macdonald Education 1982).

Journeys out of school

It is important that the whole school shares in work originating from class visits, which are often the focus for cross-curricular activities, particularly during the Summer term.

Such visits into the local neighbourhood, or to places of interest, provide valuable opportunities to develop community links, promote cultural awareness and extend children's experience beyond the confines of the school environment.

Changes to traditional family holiday arrangements mean that many children are now taken out of school during term-time. A simple but effective method of recording these excursions is the adoption of a school 'mascot' which accompanies the child on the trip. A photograph of the child and mascot taken at a place of special interest can be displayed in a prominent place in school.

Visits

The educational and social value of such trips often remains the 'property' of the group concerned. In order that the whole school can benefit from these activities, it is important for classes to report back their experiences through displays of photographs, artefacts, sketches, models, dramatised accounts of key incidents, slide or video presentations, diary extracts etc.

The leavers service

Many schools celebrate the end of the summer term with a special assembly focusing on those pupils about to set out on the next stage of their educational journey. Its contents will, of necessity, be somewhat specific but could include the following:

a)   Children's anecdotes – looking back at their best and worst memories; looking forward to their hopes for the future; saying thank you.

> *Thank you for the seasons*
> *As they swiftly come and go;*
> *For the special days of summer*
> *And sudden winter snow.*
> *Thank you for the beauty*
> *Of the distant, misty hills;*
> *For the trees in springtime glory*
> *And joyful daffodils.*
> *Thank you so for those I love*
> *And the love they give to me;*
> *For all I've learned, for all I am,*
> *And all I hope to be.*
> *Thank you so for all my life,*
> *For the laughter, hope and care;*
> *For all the times when you were close –*
> *This is my thank-you prayer.*

> *Heather Watson*
> *(Studfall Junior School, Corby)*

b)   Acknowledgement of individual and collective contributions – awards for achievement, covering a range of activities including academic, sporting, artistic, musical, environmental, and also qualities such as school spirit and endeavour.

One more step

With a spring

2. Round the corners of the world I turn,
   More and more about the world I learn.
   And the new things that I see
   You'll be looking at along with me.
   Chorus

3. As I travel through the bad and good,
   Keep me travelling the way I should.
   Where I see no way to go,
   You'll be telling me the way, I know.
   Chorus

4. Give me courage when the world is
      rough,
   Keep me loving though the world is tough.
   Leap and sing in all I do,
   Keep me travelling along with you.
   Chorus

5. You are older than the world can be,
   You are younger than the life in me.
   Ever old and ever new,
   Keep me travelling along with you.
   Chorus

Words and music by Sydney Carter

Index